CAUGHT BETWEEN CULTURES

CAUGHT BETWEEN CULTURES:
A Story Of
Milton Wan & Vietnam

Joseph Blondo

Eloquent Books
Durham, Connecticut

Eloquent Books
An imprint of Strategic Book Group
P. O. Box 333
Durham, CT 06422
http://www.StrategicBookGroup.com

ISBN: 978-1-60860-836-2

Photo Credit: Peter Mumford
Cover Illustration: Frank Morgan
Book Design: Julius Kiskis

Printed in the United States of America
17 16 15 14 13 12 11 10 09   1 2 3 4 5

Dedication

To the Immigrant—may you succeed and prosper

Dedication

Contents

Foreword

A book, any book, has a purpose, a reason for its existence. Even a book as simple and straight forward as a Hardy Boys mystery, written just for a child's sheer enjoyment, shares an embryonic impetus and motive for being born upon the blank page. Originally I thought I was solely writing the biographical story of an individual. As I proceeded along I found other voices and stories calling out to me, very persistently laying claim to this book, in unison shouting "this is our book too!" "Don't forget me, I am also important," they repeatedly said.

After listening to this unruly and troublesome crowd, too loud to be ignored I became convinced that they must be included, sometimes feeling that they and not Milton Wan were the real story here. This not only created a personal dilemma, it radically changed and altered my purpose. I found that this book could no longer focus on one person as all around him there were many compelling themes asking to be touched upon and examined. The voices of change and turmoil were in the air from the first minutes of Milton's birth, shouted from the streets of Saigon and jungles of Vietnam. They were his historical background, the daily headlines hawked by the newspaper vendors. These vociferous voices, by sheer weight and magnitude pushed and shoved themselves onto these pages making this book the one you will be reading.

I can make no apology for this. In this case the factual demands to be told, not shutting up, saying I will not be forgotten or covered up. The factual says please display me in all my arrogant ugliness and stupidity. This book is my response, the story held in your hands. This is a swift and honest non-fictional examination of an age and era resonating into the new century. That much of the same nonsense continues is something I can not fail to point out.

I end this brief foreword with one question. Why is it that the human species continues to formulate and practice polices and actions guaranteeing its demise and exit from our planet? On that somber note I leave you to enjoy and ponder the following pages.

Acknowledgments

As with every effort, literary and otherwise, there are always the behind-the-scene places and individuals that have made major contributions, without of course this book would not exist, or at least in a very different form.

To begin with, I wish to thank the Aurora, Colorado, Mobile Library "Bookmobile" and the librarians therein parked on the east side of the Altura Drugstore in the summers of 1963 and 1964 for introducing me to books and the joy of reading. Without their invaluable encouragement I would be a far different person today.

Another library I would be remiss in not mentioning is the staff of that great building and institution, Saint Deiniol's Residential Library located in the village of Hawarden, Northern Wales. It is there that the first words of this book were put on page, Saint Deiniol's forever remaining a sanctuary in my sometimes troubled mind, a place I often mentally return to when needing to flee the mundane and modern world. Where else could one be writing in serenity and quietude, surrounded by a multitude of wonderful books, and resting just inches away from your left elbow is an original first edition written by a crazed Muggletonian? No other place on this planet that I know of. Just how high is the earth's ceiling?

A third very important library in my life was the Bishop Piche School Library run by the Canadian Grey Order of Roman Catholic Sisters in Fort Chipewyan, Alberta, Canada, 1964-66, feeding me book after book. It was there that for the first time I read two books in one day. My only regret is that I don't remember the good Sisters' names but I easily recall their smiles. Thanks for assisting an earnest but confused lad.

A tip of the writing hat is required to Willie Morris for inspiration concerning description, Sinclair Lewis for social and cultural inclusion, J. B. Priestley for long sentences and fat paragraphs, and H.G. Wells for mixing political commentary into related prose.

Without Melody A's editing and extremely helpful notations this book would have remained a partial disaster until I had awakened from my haze and slumber. Many thanks!

A grateful nod to Frank Morgan for his cover artwork, and one day, who knows, we may even discover the original disc.

Another nod for Peter Mumford and your various photographs making the book complete. I just wish your camera had been ready when I leaped upon the Tai Tung counter. It would have been wonderful to have captured Tommy's expression!

And I must make note of my indebtedness to my old rock & roll buddy Jake Widman for the second editing. And yes, you are correct. I certainly love my commas and when-are-they-ever-going-to-end sentences!

Lastly, I would like to mention Tai Tung's wait staff, past and present, who have served me at least 3,500 meals and still counting. Some may not believe this but I am probably underestimating the many times I've sat at that counter or back in one of those cozy booths. So thanks again to Milton, Michael, Alan, Jimmy, Bee, Peter, Eddy, Simon, Brian, Ling, Ricky, Johnny, James, Tommy, Al and Harry. And I can't forget all the cooks, too!

Introduction

Welcome to an oral history, now transformed into biography, one that probably wouldn't have been written if it hadn't been for my bumping into said Mister Wan while eating my usual tofu and something at the Tai Tung Chinese restaurant, a favorite joint located in the middle of Seattle's Chinatown. The address, if you are interested, is 655 S. King, almost the southeast corner of Maynard Avenue S. & S. King Street, in case you ever find yourself hungry before or after a Seahawks or Sounders or Mariners game, or perhaps visiting the Wing Luke Museum just up the street, which of course you should do.

As you might guess, and possibly surmise, it's probably not usual for a commonplace waiter, or anyone similar, to have their biography, their life story recorded or written. For why should they, at least for the reasons normally given why a life is set down on paper? For most diners, and readers, it would be simply, "Give me my chow mein and let me finish eating, why don't ya anyway! Who do think you are!?" That is the question I attempt to answer in the following pages. Just who is Milton Wan and what has been his life story?

The usual biographical subject it seems is usually someone foremost in the public eye and lexicon, notable for this glorious achievement or that notorious crime, the clamoring public salivating for all the juiciest details. The sexual escapades of the rich and famous, a recent millionaire New York governor for instance, spike special interest—who did what to whom, and why? Or if there is an earthquake or forest fire, the question becomes, who was brave or not in the face of destruction and calamity? We live in an era where rumor and gossip and hyperbole is the norm: peek-a-boo, who and how are you, and how could you? Given that prevalent reality, at first glance writing about Milton Wan might seem as relevant as noting when and if your neighbor takes out the garbage. The local alley cats and marauding crows may care but why should you? The obvious point is, that until you ask or inquire, what appeared initially boring isn't at all, a few minutes investigation suddenly highly rewarding.

All this a preamble to why I was drawn to this project. From the very beginning I found Milton's story, his early years in Saigon, extremely interesting, not just entertaining but also instructive: local history, psychology, the complex interplay between Saigon's Chinese and Vietnamese communities, and much more playing leading roles in his very personal human drama featuring his misbegotten self caught in a web of circumstances not wholly of his own manufacture.

Briefly, Milton Wan's story, before anything else it might be, is one of paternal abuse, and how that evolved into a personal search for a healing acceptance, a grueling physical and psychological journey grasping for an unkind father's approval. Milton's baleful yearning reminds me of V.S. Naipaul's sad fictional character, Mister Biswas. Biswas of course was longing for a house, a mansion based upon an undying desire and dream. Similarly, Milton's emotionally distant father represented fealty and home, with both Biswas and Milton traveling beyond common sense to ultimately reach their goal. Again, how and why that happened, and his final vindication, is Milton's story and this book.

This story also recounts in part a period of Vietnamese history that's forever gone, never to be retrieved, though many Vietnamese immigrants remain in denial, still clutching that yellow South Vietnamese flag, no longer merely a banner but instead a kind of billowing talisman that will somehow magically bring back a bygone era. Just as South Vietnam as a country and political entity has vanished, so is the particular cultural setting that Milton knew also gone, this story a quick, intimate peek at a chapter closed but not completely forgotten, certainly remembered by those who can not forget a sometimes unfair history.

I have emphasized the term story, in the title and elsewhere, because as much as possible, that's what this book is, both a small snapshot of Vietnam's long narrative and Milton's very personal story, not his sibling's, nor his father's, but his alone, an intimate tale created solely from information obtained from him. Though at times severely handicapping my ability to write this book, it remains true to his initial wish: to be Milton's story, an explanation of his life, which I have strongly attempted to do. The political and cultural additions were on my initiative, feeling it necessary adding color and depth to a sometimes otherwise barren and vacant background.

Any and all omissions, therefore, are due to choice, a decision in part to adhere to Milton's wishes, because this truly is his autobiography but only written a by hand other than his own. Any thorough interview with his family members I'm sure would have provided a "treasure trove" of new information, possibly greatly altering what I have sometimes felt is a somewhat myopic view and opinion of himself and his overall situation. So out of loyalty, misplaced or not, this remains, and always will be, Milton's book, not mine. Consider then this book as what it really is, a public service rendered on behalf of a harassed soul. Given his past circumstances, it's the least I could do, both as a writer chronicling his life, and now also his steadfast friend.

Tai Tung Restaurant, Seattle's Chinatown, International District.

One

Vietnam 1943 and Childhood: Milton and Michael's Unexplainable Persecution

In 1943, the year Milton Wan and his twin brother Michael were born; Vietnam and Southeast Asia were very different places from the ones presented to us over American television in the 1960s. Politically, the artificial divide that became North and South Vietnam, partitioning a people behind an imaginary polemical border, did not exist, waiting to be created. Saigon, now renamed Ho Chi Minh City, Milton and Michael's birthplace, was then known as the capital city of the colonial creation known as Cochinchina, the southernmost part of a greater French Indochina, which also included the ancient kingdoms of Laos and Cambodia. Vietnam itself had been further divided by the French into two other regions, the middle or central section named Annam, with Hue, Vietnam's ancient imperial capital, as its primary city, now unfortunately known as one of the bloodiest battle sites of the Vietnam conflict. The northernmost province was Tonkin, featuring Hanoi as its major city, now of course the capital city of a now united and Communist Vietnam.

By the way, if you find the name Tonkin somewhat familiar, a dim intrusive memory, it's probably due to the now infamous Gulf of Tonkin incident occurring off the coast of Vietnam, President Johnson accusing North Vietnam of attacking two

1

American Navy destroyers, the *Maddox* and the *C. Turner Joy*, in neutral waters. I use the term infamous, because historically it now appears to be something that never happened, certainly not in the manner described at the time. Nonetheless, Johnson used the alleged insult to justify a massive escalation by the United States, expanding what was essentially a civil war into a much larger ideological confrontation.

Milton and Michael's birth coincided with a particularly tumultuous and traumatic period in Vietnam's history, simultaneously occupied not by one but by two foreign powers, the Vichy French and the Imperial Japanese. The Vichy were the remnants of a broken nation, part of France's 1940 defeat and capitulation to a belligerent Nazi Germany. The Vichy were led by Marshal Petain, a French hero dating from WW I, who were allowed, under watchful supervision by Germany, to nominally govern and administrate Vichy (unoccupied) France and most of its overseas territories.

Japan's encroachment upon the Asian mainland, largely justified by a desire for natural resources required by a growing industrial base, began in the late nineteenth century, China being a primary target. The menace of the "Yellow Tide," highlighted for most Americans by Japan's unprovoked assault upon the US territory of Hawaii in December 1941, had been in reality attacking and overwhelming its nearest neighbors for years, French Indochina being one of Japan's many victims. Given Vichy France's collaboration with Germany, transforming France from adversary to nominal ally, Japan took on the role as a kind of silent partner, allowing France to maintain their colonial rule. That uneasy alliance ended suddenly in April 1945, when a French revolt against the Japanese failed, the insurrection quashed by the Imperial Army.

Unfortunately for Vietnam, foreign occupation and internal manipulation were not unusual circumstances, its roughly two-thousand-year history tainted by an almost unabated legacy of foreign dominance and interference, the various Chinese Dynasties guilty of a near perpetual and brutal enslavement of the noncompliant Vietnamese.

Milton owes his Vietnamese birthplace to his paternal grandfather, a Chinese banker from Shanghai who immigrated to Saigon around 1908, one year after Milton's father, Wainam, was born. One could probably say that the grandfather's migration was only a continuation of that two-millennium-long invasion, an individual incursion into a sovereign nation.

An important notation is that Milton knows little concerning his grandparents' personal history or his parents' childhood, for instance, not knowing where his paternal grandmother was born or raised, despite spending much of his childhood living with her. I bring this up to highlight the mystery associated with Milton's childhood, something you will hear much more about. Sometimes I feel that there was, or is a kind of "conspiracy of silence," every detail and element of the Wan family a guarded secret, a kind of domestic cabal. Though it may be true that this is simply a Chinese cultural trait, and not wholly confined to the Wan clan, I will never understand why it isn't reasonable to have a workable knowledge of one's own family, given the primary position the family unit holds in traditional Chinese societal structure.

Many of my questions directed to Milton went unanswered because simply he didn't know. I could never tell whether the Wans were intensely private, or perhaps somehow inherently taciturn, a silent, internally mute family, economical with speech, idle talk deemed unnecessary commentary upon the obvious. The "fictional mystery," that well known best selling literary form, at least always holds a key to the locked door that, upon opening, reveals all to the startled audience.

In Milton's case, something which is very real and nonfictional, I remain staring at that damn door, wondering just what exists behind; and after repeatedly rattling the handle, questioning why it remains locked and sealed. I hope this explains my sometimes unintended brevity, just simply not having enough information to draw from. If this were a novelistic portrayal of a family or era, like Galsworthy's great *Forsyte Saga*, there wouldn't be a problem just making things up, though obviously, nonfiction does not allow that kind of creativity and literary freedom though I have been tempted.

What Milton does know is that his father returned to Shanghai as a teenager to attend high school, later moving on to Canton (now modern Guangzhou) and the local university, majoring in a number of foreign languages, including English. Again, without any information detailing how and why, Wainam was in Hong Kong where he met his future wife, Olga Jung, a Chinese-American exchange student from Los Angeles, California. Sometime in the early 1930s, they married, settling in Shanghai in 1935. Soon thereafter, their first son Frederick was born.

Sometime in 1936 the young family moved to Paris, France, Wainam having been appointed as first secretary to the Chinese ambassador to France, the ambassador a friend from university days. Again, more unanswered questions. There exists the clear implication that Wainam was accustomed to social privilege, the lofty heights of Chinese and Vietnamese society familiar, perhaps even commonplace, knowing ambassadors the norm rather than some exceptional circumstance. Superiority and hubris appear to be important emotional components in his attitude toward life in particular and to others in general, including his own family. How helpful it would have been to be more extensively informed about Milton's parents. In part, I feel like I'm guessing, which I think is my own overreaction, but nonetheless the feeling remains.

Unfortunately, after about four years in Paris, Wainam was forced to resign, this happening sometime in 1940, during the early stages of WW II. The prevailing rumor or myth is that he was caught embezzling embassy funds. What isn't rumor were Wainam's first stages of a lifelong, chronic history with alcohol abuse, his temper and behavior suddenly flaring, always a potential firestorm. There were also hints of ongoing infidelities. The career foundation he had created was now beginning to erode and disappear, an unavoidable byproduct of his instability. Adding to the mix and complexity were the birth of two more children, Edmond in 1937, and in 1939, their first daughter Victoria. All of this was complicated by the spreading war. The Germans occupied Paris on June 13, 1940. It wasn't realistic to remain in such an uncertain and chaotic environment, especially after losing his diplomatic immunity. They would have to leave but where was the question at hand.

One would think, at least I do, that moving to the United States would have been the logical choice, Olga's American origin and citizenship hopefully facilitating a quick entry. They might have been considered legitimate war refugees if they had only applied. All I do know is that Wainam Wan chose a very interesting time to return to Vietnam. The Japanese were fighting in French Indochina. China and Japan were officially at war. It seems odd that he would trade one war zone for another. Los Angeles, California, Olga's home town, was an obviously safer destination. Nevertheless, sometime in 1941, the Wan family made it to Saigon, the details of their amazing journey across a warring world unknown, at least to Milton. Shortly after their arrival, the last daughter, Marie, was born. The twins arrived two years later in October 1943.

Maybe Wainam's return was prompted by simple economics, feeling that the expanding war created new money-making opportunities. It's not a new concept. His father was a banker, a leading figure in Saigon's financial community. He must have received encouragement from someone to make such a daring trek across a turbulent world. Possibly he felt admonished by his failure in France, going back home his only true chance for a complete redemption. Whatever his motivation, he had immersed his family in a political and cultural cauldron, a miasmatic quicksand inundating all who entered, regardless of background and position. This would be Milton's childhood playground, a contradictory, neurotic society focused upon blind self-destruction; a pantomime with imaginary playmates, war and political imperatives the cultural guiding hand.

Given what little Milton knows concerning his family's early Saigon years, much of what I write for the next few paragraphs should be considered educated guesswork, and that's a guess in and of itself. Milton thinks his father's initial years back in Saigon were mired in financial failure, creating the superstition that Milton and Michael were responsible for their ensuing hardships, explaining the abusive treatment later directed toward his twin sons. In short, Milton's hypothesis is that the twins were blamed for their father's monetary difficulties, their birth seen as an ill omen presaging disaster. It is true that they alone, amongst all the children, were singled out for the intolerable treatment outlined in this book.

It also appears to be true that Samuel's birth, 1947 in Saigon, and overall childhood, was the opposite side of the lucky coin, beginning, according to Milton, a period of great family prosperity. Sam's birth then was equated with good fortune, the luck of the Chinese if not of the Irish. The only trouble with this theory is that Milton doesn't know if they actually were poor during this four year period because he doesn't remember it, and of course has never received any corroborating evidence from his siblings. What this theory really appears to be is an attempt at explaining the unexplainable. What their father's inexplicable behavior appears to display is a pronounced inability to reconcile their birth. Soon you will begin to understand what I mean, and why to this day Milton remains puzzled. Above all the other good reasons, his father's horrendously bad behavior is why this book was written.

During this transition period for Milton's family, Vietnam ostensibly remained under Japanese occupation until the final armistice was signed on September 2, 1945, aboard the American battleship USS *Missouri*, finally ending what was termed the Pacific Theater, thus closing that most costly chapter of world history, WW II. Interestingly, the final resistance in Vietnam against the Japanese was provided by Ho Chi Minh and the Vietnamese underground fighters, these very same forces the genesis of the army that fought the French in the 1950s, and then of course the Americans twenty years later.

Unlike the European Theater resistance movements, like the French and Yugoslav who eventually got their countries back, the Vietnamese were not so lucky. Instead, post-WW II Vietnam was not granted a much deserved independence, unfortunately falling victim to new Cold War geopolitical maneuvering; maintaining a continuation of what at least theoretically WW II was intended to end: the foreign occupation of sovereign nations. Vietnam's pleas for national autonomy were given a deaf ear, completely and utterly ignored by an arrogant "Western World" community, the United States and Europe holding an agenda limited in its vision and scope. I need to mention that all of this might have been different had Franklin Delano Roosevelt survived further into his fourth term. As early as 1943 he was making supportive statements concerning Vietnam's post-war independence. Another factor could have been the change in vice-presidents, Henry Wallace far more progressive that Harry Truman. It shows how history can be dictated by the proverbial rolling-of-the-dice.

The united Allied powers decreed that Indochina, including Vietnam, should remain a French colony, that decision being the "final discussion." The Vietnamese, especially the resistance fighters, were not pleased. This poorly considered and flawed stance, made worse by America's intervention after France's defeat and ouster in the mid-1950s, directly translated into the expanding conflict that consumed the 1960s, internally devouring Vietnam until reaching a final numbing conclusion (at least for the Americans), in 1975.

The justification voiced for all this future destruction was that it was done for the greater good for all the world's nations. By defeating the Communist scourge here and now, it would send the strongest message, a dire warning to anyone contemplating such insolence. Following this line of thinking, popularized in part by George Kennan's very influential 1947 article encouraging the containment of Soviet Communism, the theory went that by stopping a particular political domino from toppling, all other potential victims would remain standing, and most importantly free and untainted from poisonous Marxist/Leninist doctrines.

Fast-forwarding to the current year of 2009, this spurious argument made all the more fallacious by events since 1975: the demise of the Soviet Union, the breaking apart of the Yugoslav Federation, and the spreading "globalization" embracing all nations regardless of ideological stance. What Presidents Eisenhower, Kennedy, Johnson, and Nixon all failed to understand, was that over any given time period, all nations change and adapt, nothing being "etched in political stone."

Today's China is a very good example of this kind of evolution. Though democratically far from ideal, consider the huge, dimensional changes from Mao's 1976 "Cultural Revolution" to Hu Jintao's version of free-market "Red Capitalism." Who could have imagined though as unexpected as it may seem, it is true, it happened, transformed into a functional reality read daily in our newspapers, and somewhat comically, bolstering our own financial system, once the antithesis of China's socialist dream.

So my next thought is obvious. What would Milton's Vietnam be like now minus the outside intervention and the many years of unnecessary war? I find the notion intriguing. It wasn't accidental that Vietnam was chosen for this intervention, this dubious honor. In the middle decades of the 20th century, South Vietnam and North Vietnam were relatively obscure countries that most Americans had never heard of, Indochina not a region easily located upon that colorful globe gathering dust on the living room coffee table next to that new totem of colloquial culture, the television.

Tucked away in a remote corner of Asia, maybe the "policy hawks" in Washington, D.C., thought that the American public really wouldn't notice, hoping that a swift, surgically clean military operation would quickly quiet the enemy, at worst the war remembered as a secondary, historical footnote. This may seem naïve now but the United States, throughout its 200-year-plus history, and especially in its own "hemisphere of influence," has repeatedly and successfully involved itself in various kinds of military actions, vindicating the use of military might.

President Johnson himself, in the midst of the Vietnam conflict, on April 27, 1965, ordered the invasion of the Dominican Republic, bringing a rapid conclusion to a burgeoning civil war. And on October 25, 1983, Ronald Reagan had his own Caribbean adventure. Under the guise of rescuing a handful of American medical students, the US invaded the tiny island nation of Grenada, skirmishing against a handful of Cuban engineers building an airport.

An intriguing coincidence is that it was the same individual, Wesley L. McDonald, who, having first led the initial retaliatory bombing against North Vietnam, found himself eighteen years later guiding "Operation Fury," as the invasion of Grenada was known. Two for two isn't bad if you are going for unjustified incursions. Must be some kind of record, something they issue medals for plus also guaranteeing that your death is published in the *New York Times*, which is where I found this obscure tidbit. Also all these years later the question can still be asked, just what was Reagan so furious about?

Of course, as in South Vietnam, these American incursions do not always succeed as planned. The March 18, 2003, invasion of Iraq, George W. Bush's "Shock & Awe" campaign, illustrates what overconfidence and poor planning will get you: a rising death toll and no clear exit from a horrific situation. Banners unfurled by the president upon the deck of an aircraft carrier symbolized not victory, as it was intended but instead a serious, unbridled arrogance tied to wishful thinking, fantasy colliding with obvious reality. Unfortunately, constructive "thinking" will never be something associated with the eight years of his presidency. President Bush, as it has been suggested many times elsewhere, appears to have been a puppet maneuvered by wonkish ideologues intent upon instilling their vision of the world into governmental policy.

Some other recent military misadventures include Reagan's October 23, 1983, debacle in Beirut, Lebanon, with a loss of over 241 marines after an explosion at their barracks. Perhaps in response, and how could it be mere coincidence, his invasion of Grenada coming two days later. And who can forget Clinton's 1994 United Nations disastrous peacekeeping mission in Somalia, made especially memorable by the infamous photographs of dead marines dragged down the streets through crowds of cheering Somalis. Having made Clinton gun-shy, some historians believe that particular policy defeat is directly linked to the terrible Rwandan genocide dating that same year, Clinton understandably reluctant to enter a situation he didn't fully understand. Clinton, by the way, made a public apology for his inaction over Rwanda, but as his apologies come too easily, his sincerity must be questioned if not completely disbelieved.

Vietnam then was just another gross political miscalculation, the United States underestimating the resolution of an oppressed people, with over two million Vietnamese needlessly killed. In reality, the Vietnamese people were an afterthought, their wants and desires given very little consideration. As I have said, their country was one just part of a much larger global scenario and political agenda. Political justifications always continue to amaze me, condoning unimaginable behaviors, worse than any horror film, Vietnam another pawn in a very ruthless game.

Milton's earliest memories begin at about age six, which

roughly brings his personal history quickly up to 1950. I should mention that this is a fairly late age for first memories. What unknown traumas occurred will always remain mere speculation. During this period, the final additions to the Wan family, both sons, were born: the aforementioned Samuel, in 1947; and Rodney, the only child born the United States, in 1949 in Los Angeles, during what must have been a rare visit home for Olga. This is the only reference to Olga's home country until her final departure, rejoining her children in Seattle. Wainam, meanwhile, had clearly established himself as a professional interpreter and middleman. Fluency in five languages proved an invaluable asset when negotiating complex international deals and arrangements. Milton remembers countless visits by businessmen of varying nationalities to their flat at Number 24 Ky Con Street. All the children were instructed to answer the telephone, not in Chinese but in French: "Non, Monsieur Wan n'est à la maison."

Everyone's first retained memory is usually significant, analogous to a light bulb turning on in the brain for the very first time, an event normally noted throughout a given lifetime as the first moment "I understood that I was alive." Given this red-letter importance then, Milton's initial awareness, this first awakening to life, can best be described as nightmarish, finding himself in a kind of familial apartheid, a palpable, invisible barrier separating the twins from the family core. Their father apparently viewed the both of them with a profound disregard, or more correctly a hatred astonishing in its intensity. In short, they were pariahs, subjected to an internal banishment, strangely exiled from their home family. The twins, Milton had discovered, had been assigned the role of external satellites orbiting though never touching the planetary surface that was their parents and siblings. It was a first memory not in the usual sense. It was anguished, an extreme agitation, a coloring black. To say the least it was a profound and disappointing recognition that something was terribly wrong.

Rare wedding portrait of Milton's parents—Shanghai 19___

Family portrait Saigon early 1950s. That is Milton standing to the left of his father.

Early family portrait mid-1940s, Milton sitting to right of his father.

Unfortunately, this noxious environment poisoned Milton. For reasons unknown or call it a kind of good luck, Michael was innately far more immune to his father's venom, better able at deflecting his unbridled malevolence. That can't be said of Milton. In a true sense, he became a prisoner, jailed by his father's attitude, serving a sentence for a crime never committed, and even worse, feeling guilty, a weighty burden not reconciled until many years later. On more than one occasion, his father jeered that if he had only known at Milton's birth what he was going to be he would have squeezed him to death. Not quite the affectionate message one might anticipate but for the twins this kind of vitriol typical, commonplace, what they now expected to hear, their father having become the enemy, someone to fear and avoid. In a word, they were at his mercy. And when he was drunk he became a monster, his fury unrelenting.

Odious behavior, certainly, though as I've said, fairly pointless to continue discussing why because we'll never truly know, at this juncture the reasons are to a large degree superfluous. What will always remain important was the impact upon Milton, he being the story, his father a very irritating addendum.

Wainam's behavior doesn't change, instead only going from bad to worse, writing his own very personal definition of a profound malignancy affecting everyone around him. In summation, he wasn't a happy man. His personality, his psychological makeup, was conflicted. On one side, an innate insecurity; then conversely an overbearing arrogance compensating for his inadequacy, a distorted equilibrium somehow balanced by too much whiskey. Not only was he discontented, he was extremely confused, bewilderment layered upon unhappiness, his internal life a series of seismic events, emotional fault lines shifting this direction and that, resulting in internal tremors, a human upheaval knocking Milton over and down. Upon entering the flat, the floor trembled, the very foundation sensing catastrophe. Father was home, and if you couldn't run, you had better hide.

Viewed broadly, Wainam's attitude toward his entire family was unquestionably mixed, ranging from benign neutrality to overt favoritism. What his feelings were concerning Olga are again a mystery, but there are suggestions of a dramatic deterioration occurring sometime around 1953, she essentially disappearing from the active running of the household, with her oldest daughters taking on her usual role. Olga was busy elsewhere, having opened a restaurant with a close girlfriend. This business relationship later expanded into a sole proprietorship, greatly financing her children's emigration to the United States. It is clear that she knew she wasn't getting any help from her husband.

Around this same period, Wainam had established a second part-time residence, occupied full-time by his mistress and her child, and oddly enough, occasionally by Samuel, who had somehow evolved into the star child. This awkward and potentially explosive situation might explain Olga's decision to cut her losses and create a life outside of her marriage. Though ultimately the advantages outweighed the negatives, Olga obviously feeling she had little alternative or negotiating power with her implacable, incendiary husband, Wainam's pronouncements always the final agenda, the constitution governing their marriage.

Fortunately for Milton, Ky Con Street served as a safe haven outside of the uncertainty that was his home life, an usually quiet and shady lane, trees lining both sides of the street, the local children using the asphalt roadway as their convenient playground. A rare ethnic harmony and mix prevailed in the neighborhood, Chinese and Vietnamese peacefully sharing the same street. China's twenty-century-long occupation of Vietnam had created what was now a traditional distrust and lingering animosity, the separation between the two groups at times palpable. One sore point was Chinese dominance in the local banking industry, their societal position similar to one once held by various European Jewish communities in pre-WW II Europe, simultaneously respected and resented. That sentiment was markedly absent from Ky Con, Milton sharing the neighborhood with his Vietnamese playmates, kicking balls, petting the puppies from the guard dog kennel, all the while speaking Vietnamese, not his native Cantonese.

Ky Con's relative residential, middle-class atmosphere was nicely balanced by a wide array of businesses serving both the local families and the hordes of day laborers and fishermen passing down the street to the nearby river. A cafe serving coffee opened at four in the morning. A bakery worthy of Paris provided the workers with baguettes and croissants golden and soft. A shop's pungent aroma of fermenting soy sauce engulfed the early morning air, intermingling with the strong odor of freshly caught fish from fishmonger stalls a block away. Sometimes shouts from the fishermen unloading their catches awakened Milton in the deep black of morning, the whispered conversations of passing workers a soft, indecipherable murmur. As dawn arrived, fruit and vegetable vendors opened their portable stalls, Ky Con no longer merely residential but now transformed into a living and stridently vocal grocery store.

This unique panorama formed the background, the scenery and flavor for Milton's earliest years, an approximate two-square-block area his initial stomping grounds, just two blocks away from his paternal grandparent's house. Other than rare housemaid-escorted excursions to see the traveling Chinese opera troupes from Hong Kong, which Milton still favors, Ky Con and the flat was his early vision of the world.

Imagine your average railroad boxcar, just a little bit longer and wider but nearly twice as tall, then you'll successfully get a rough idea approximating the actual physical dimensions of #24 Ky Con. Stylistically, the buildings lining both sides of Ky Con share an identical design, bearing a strong similarity to San Francisco's Victorian-style row houses, though displaying a strong, local French colonial accent and flair, the second story flats sharing very distinctive, connecting verandas, reminiscent of New Orleans and the American Deep South. Being tall, the buildings create a kind of urban canyon, the street surface below a dry riverbed, the blue sky above a looming heaven.

Situated at street level, #24 fronts the street, the door opening wide to wandering pedestrians and miscellaneous debris and rubbish left over from the morning vendors. Stepping inside, and shutting out the street, a magical spaciousness awaits you: like a conjurer's trick, what appears small is suddenly a great immensity, twenty-foot high ceilings, and toward the rear, a loft-style bedroom reached by a staircase. Two large floor-level bedrooms provided ample sleeping areas for the children. The Wan's two maids had individual sleeping quarters attached to the kitchen, large but a bit of a tight fit for twelve potential diners rubbing elbows and chop sticks. At times, #24 was a delightful mixture of domestic commotion and shouting children, maids and daughters in furious motion, laughter bouncing off the tall ceilings. Those were the good moments.

When Wainam arrived home, this ofttimes quickly changed, especially when drunk. Suddenly remembering the twins' great offense, he would beat them with an especially reserved paddle, making sure they would never forget what they never knew to begin with, the twins frightened mice, their father the vengeful cat. With the establishment of his second residence, these incidents slowly diminished to only the occasional insult, knowing there must be limitations short of actual murder. Even Wainam understood the advantages of restraint.

When all the Wan children came of age, yes even the twins, they were sent to an "all-Chinese" school, a segregated bastion of Chinese exclusionism: the Ling Nam Academy, nominally run by the Chinese Baptist Church, teaching American Christian moralism but with a decidedly Chinese and Confucian tilt, an odd mixture of ethnic patriotic nostalgia, filial piety, and a stern "Jesus is going to eat you if you are not careful." Simply, Ling Nam's mission was to instill modified militaristic values and discipline into the already fairly compliant student body, preparing them for a cultural inheritance far more than middle-class, it becoming their anointed duty defending the ramparts against all alien inclusions.

More than merely a school, in reality Ling Nam was a socially insular factory whose main product, above anything else it might have produced, for instance, broadening education, was party-line conformity, the issuing of invisible ethnic purity identification cards ensuring order within the marching ranks. Ling Nam's statement was simple, that Chinese superiority was implicit, as natural as the sky above and the ground below, with a smiling Baptist God (with an assenting nod from Confucius) beneficently looking down, blessing all good work and effort.

Having personally walked around the building that was once

Ling Nam Academy, I found it to be an impressive and imposing structure. Taken in total, adding up the school building and dormitories and grounds, you have an extensive property taking up two square blocks, a living personification of the philosophy that spawned it, Ling Lam obviously once the neighborhood bully, pushy and arrogant, like Milton's father, daring the world to push back!

Tall beige brick walls, three to four stories high, are bordered with green tiles, with matching tiles for the many roofs, keeping the passing world and weather out, and in the 1950s, the many boys and girls, with matching uniforms, in. The interior complex was vast, a self-contained universe encompassing a gymnasium, many basketball courts and a soccer field; built-in entertainment for the energetic hordes bored with classes. Feeding the now-ravenous girls and boys were busy cooks in industrial-size kitchens serving up steamed rice and spicy tofu in the spacious cafeteria and dining area, an orderly maze of interlacing tables and long benches, the children a tidal surge pouring into the hall.

Milton's attitude toward Ling Lam was divided, parallel to his emotions concerning himself, a strong like and dislike, both needing and hating Ling Nam, equally loving and hating himself, enjoying the school's youthful camaraderie, at the same time despising a perceived neglect and exclusion. This division of mind and heart was unfortunately reinforced by the academy's headmaster who just so happened to be Wainam's former college classmate, whose behavior toward the twins was little better than their father's, a surrogate bully mirroring Wainam's aversion, wagging his finger, shaking his head, for good measure rapping their knuckles, assuring that he wouldn't be misunderstood. Milton felt both wronged and shamed. Whatever he had done, it must have been pretty awful to deserve this treatment. And similarly, like at home, he was trapped, nowhere to run nor hide, left no other option than suffering in silence, complaint only bringing further punishment and retribution.

The twins were always day students, meaning living outside the school, except for a two-year hiatus between 1953 and 1955, when Ling Nam's dormitories served as their home. Milton's description of those two years is reminiscent of something out of Charles Dickens' *David Copperfield*, mid-nineteenth-century England suddenly incarnate: Ling Nam's dormitory life an austere and joyless regimen, the daily routine a plodding tic-toc, tic-toc punctuality marking the day; the school master a new Chinese Mister Creakle making sure Milton counted each second of a given hour—Ling Nam now Salem House.

Ling Nam's day began promptly at seven in the morning; the lights automatically turned and kept on, discouraging any and all sleepy heads, the boys pouring into the shower rooms for their mandatory, communal bathing, shouting and squealing kept to a minimum please! After thoroughly drying and quickly yet carefully dressing themselves, everyone proceeded to the long wooden tables and benches in the immense dining hall, a large painting of a European (and white) Jesus looming over them, reminding to be ever thankful for their never altered breakfast of congee (also known as rice porridge or jook), the Chinese equivalent to the American morning oatmeal, plus a plain hum bow and pickled radishes.

Of course, no talking was allowed during this serious, nutritive undertaking, quiet chewing a ruminating murmur until a clanging bell announced breakfast's end and the beginning of morning classes. Lunch and afternoon classes and dinner continued in similar fashion, evening reserved for study and some playtime. Weekends were a dull monotony, with church and various devotionals being the primary diversions.

Weekends at Ling Nam were particularly hellish for Milton, for unlike the other boys and girls who either went home or had weekend visits from their families bearing gifts and treats, the twins never had any visitors, let alone presents, except for one solitary occasion when their sister Victoria surprised them. That was it for two entire years, no letters, no telephone calls, and not one visit from their parents. During Ling Nam's summer closure, instead of going home, they lived with their grandparents. This unexplained pattern of segregation and silence from their family continued for four years until 1959, when the twins were finally allowed to return to Ky Con street.

During this four-year long sequester the visits home were rare though just a couple of blocks away. My guess is that Olga and Wainam were at some kind of extreme marital impasse concerning the twins, something that took years to resolve. As usual, Milton and Michael paying the highest price, shoved aside and nearly forgotten, imprisoned for their unknown crime.

Though at times enjoying his two dormitory years, a negative imprint deepened in an already fragile psyche. The estrangement he felt from his greater family circle transferred over to formal society itself, the message now interpreted as an innate inferiority: Milton and Michael being less, never more, permanently dysfunctional beings undeserving of affection and respect.

Ling Nam's interesting blend of Christianity and Confucianism, preaching filial piety and unswerving obedience worked against Milton's personal sense of psychological integrity and autonomy. How could he disrespect his father when everything and everyone around him told him differently, instinctively telling him that disobedience was a sin, loyalty coming first, your personal needs a distant second. The question posed for Milton was how to love a father who relentlessly abused him. As you'll soon see, his initial youthful response was confused and contradictory, pressing, pushing him into a corner.

In real terms, Milton's quandary remains extant to this day as he has never discovered a final resolution to his father's treatment, a lingering incoherency at times prompting some very questionable responses. Of course, fidelity as an ideal is admirable, but in this case unfortunately deadly. His experiences at Ling Nam compounded an unreasonable guilt, already weighty, into something crushing. All of this more than unfair, it was clearly criminal but what could a little boy do—there was nothing he could do.

As if it was necessary, further insult was Wainam's habitual delinquency concerning their tuition. Curious and unfortunate but perhaps predictable behavior, the continuation of a lamentable theme, sung without any foreseeable expiration. Wainam was simply being cruel. Without question Samuel and Rodney's tuition was always promptly paid. This glaring discrepancy was made a public issue, the principal openly taunting the twins, their disgrace now part of a shameful curriculum, a new kind of moral lesson. It seemed there was no escape but an unintentional kind of clemency occurred in 1959 when the South Vietnamese government of President Diem began curtailing Ling Nam's educational activities, first shutting the dormitories down. A year later the school was permanently closed, signaling the end of a local era.

Simultaneously around this time, American influence had greatly increased, possibly emboldening the Vietnamese to expand their own cultural agenda, Ling Nam's inclusive xenophobia not compatible within a country struggling with its own identity and real survival. Ling Nam obviously was a cultural dinosaur, a living anachronism doomed to a timely extinction, a museum piece relinquished to memory, a malignancy that had to be removed, the refractory resident Chinese reluctantly merged into the greater South Vietnamese society.

As for Milton, he had remained essentially dormant, locked away in a kind of emotional hibernation, or worse, a living coma; or using a psychiatric allusion, a catatonic state, perfectly able to hear everything around him yet paralyzed, physically unable to respond. This was Milton's life, a neutralized existence, without real and viable connection. However purposely or not, Wainam had achieved his goal, rendering Milton invisible to himself while simultaneously feeling very much alive. Having now reached adolescence, he truly had no idea on how to proceed, having only experienced a rigid control, not the loving guidance so necessary to create a viable internal compass taking him into mature adulthood. Milton was a young man adrift, destined toward immoveable masses, bumping against obvious realities, his only option to blindly go forward, his theme clearly spelled out. The going would not be easy.

Two

Adolescence: Father Louie & Working in the Hotels

The ending of the 1950s meant far more to the Republic of South Vietnam than a mere numerical change in decades. For what had begun in the late 1950s, the first hints of a civil war, not to mention North Vietnam's interference with South Vietnam's internal affairs, the new decade would become a frightening, chaotic period of unparalleled destruction costing millions of Vietnamese lives, and ultimately, the demise of South Vietnam as an independent political state. Serious American involvement began during the latter stages of President Eisenhower's administration, sending economic assistance and the first of many military advisors to South Vietnam. It would be interesting to know if Eisenhower ever imagined that his initial gestures would suddenly explode into the fiasco the war ultimately became.

I am again unfortunately reminded of a similar miscalculation, with President George W. Bush's decision to invade Iraq in March 2003, actually believing the American forces would be welcomed by cheering crowds tossing flowers, somehow a glorious replication of the Allied Forces' celebrated 1944 liberation of Paris. The Sunni insurgency and the other violent actions over the course of six years tragically dispelling any and all such foolish notions, with over 4,330 American lives taken and the counting ongoing. The Iraqi government has just released a study stating that over 100,000 civilians have been killed since the American intervention. Am I the only one remembering that Bush promised that there would be no civilian deaths or "collateral damage" as it is sometimes called? All those Iraqis lives needlessly lost, with their fatalities increasing week by deadly week.

The new American President, Barack Obama, while campaigning, promised the American voting public that if elected he would withdraw all US troops from Iraq in sixteen months beginning from his inauguration, which would have meant sometime in May 2010. Unfortunately, since winning the presidency he has now changed his withdrawal tune to nineteen months, meaning the timetable is now August 2010. In addition to that alteration, he is planning on keeping up to 50,000 troops as advisors and trainers for how many extra years we don't know though again promising that all of them will be out by the end of 2011. It is also important to remember the continuing financial cost of the war, at its height costing the United States over 10 billon dollars a month. History may find it interesting that the newest recipient of the Nobel Peace Prize just recently proposed the largest Defense budget in American history, a tidy 607 billion dollars or possibly even more spent in a depressed economy that can ill afford such an enormous expenditure. It appears that both additional lives and taxpayer dollars are considered expendable regardless of long-term consequences.

To me, I hear an echo, hearing and looking too much like South Vietnam recycled, only for a newly trusting American audience, who like me, took Obama at his word. You can bet more soldiers will be killed after the so-called "active involvement" is over. So much for promises kept. It is highly doubtful that the additional fatalities caused by this policy switch will ever truly rest in peace. At least the dead "green card" holders now receive a postmortem gift of full legal American citizenship. Maybe it acts as a kind of passport guaranteeing swift passage through the gilded gates of Heaven.

And if this is the Department of Defense and the Pentagon's version of humane treatment and justice, I can now understand why they felt that "waterboarding" was not torture. Interestingly, Obama has decided that the CIA operatives who used this technique, which by the way is banned by the Geneva Convention, will either not be prosecuted or at least limited to a few. His justification has been that all they were doing was following Justice Department directives approving the use of waterboarding. I would certainly like to hear the opinion of those who were tortured. I'm sure it would be highly informative. Maybe they too would like to be granted American citizenship. I think they have earned it.

A sobering footnote to the Iraqi conflict is the expanding campaign to oust the Taliban in Afghanistan. During aerial bombings of Taliban positions during the first full week of May 2009, it appears that the Americans accidentally killed as many as 147 Afghani civilians, including scores of children. In September 2009 another air strike, this time called in by the Germans, killed a hundred or more noncombatants. Even though the overall goals of the current Obama presidency might seem theoretically pure, it is very difficult to justify all these innocent deaths, killing the same people you are claiming to protect. Paying families two thousand dollars per death seems a poor substitute for a living and breathing person. I doubt if Obama would consider that adequate compensation if his two daughters were part of the killed and maimed. How can this be considered a moral and just situation? The answer is too obvious. The old policy beats never end, the drum passed from administration to administration, forever killing and destroying and breaking hearts.

Outraged Afghanis are now throwing rocks at passing American and NATO convoys. The current Afghani president, Hamid Karzai, himself mired in a messy and fraudulent election, has requested a stop to all aerial attacks. It is difficult to see a positive conclusion to all of this. I can see Obama possibly becoming a 21st century version of Lyndon Baines Johnson, forging a strong domestic agenda while formulating a disaster overseas. Not a good beginning. And how and when will it end?

Though Eisenhower's ultimate contribution pales in comparison to the three subsequent administrations, he does bear responsibility for the first American fatalities, with two US Army advisors killed in an ambush near Bien Hoa, South Vietnam in July, 1959. 1960 saw the formation of the South Vietnamese Communists into an official army, calling itself the "National Liberation Front," but more popularly known as the "Vietcong" or "Vietminh." By organizing into a united front, the NLF made itself exceedingly clear to both the South Vietnamese government of Ngo Dinh Diem and the world at large that the opposition in this conflict was deadly serious and would not be easily dissuaded.

This open defiance probably wasn't the wisest decision, prompting the new American president, John Kennedy, to quickly escalate United States involvement, with a few regional allies like Australia and South Korea later joining the fray. Without Kennedy's fateful decision to widen the conflict, the war might have ended in a handful of months, especially given the rampant corruption operating within the South Vietnamese government and army—an institutionalized dysfunction so painfully obvious it was like the proverbial "betting on a dead horse." How could anyone have thought that they held an ability win a prolonged war?

It appears that American eagerness to make a strong statement against the perceived worldwide spread of Communism clouded the Kennedy administration's judgment and wisdom, because in they went, with America not getting totally out until after April 1975, and the deaths of over 58,000 Americans. The Vietnamese civil war was now an American war, providing the background for Milton's personal dilemma. Without the protracted war I'm sure the entire Wan family would have immediately immigrated to the United States, thus there being no story to write. But the war colored Milton's future, sometimes red, sometimes black, an abstract canvas turned upside down, and at odd angles too!

With Ling Nam's closure Milton was at a complete loss. Having been prepared for nothing, nothing was his response. The twins were now again residing at Ky Con Street. Again, I have no idea why the change in living arrangements. Possibly it was because there was now plenty of room. The exodus to Seattle had begun in earnest, Vicki, Marie, and Edmond joining their brother Frederick, who had departed a couple years earlier. Later in 1960, Sam would also join them, his departure leaving the twins and Rodney, the youngest, behind. Rodney left two years later, again leaving the twins in a very familiar position, marooned, isolated and bewildered.

Yes, the twins were home again, a rather Pyrrhic, or muted victory, considering all their siblings had either left or were leaving soon, but they did have a new school to attend, another type of religious school focusing on the English language, Father Louie's "Pacific Academy," run by a Chinese-American Catholic priest. Unusual, you say? Not when you know that he was a close friend and advisor to President Diem, who was as widely known for his intense devotion to the Catholic Church as for anything remotely administrative. In the government's view, Ling Nam and the Pacific Academy were as different as sunny afternoons versus the darkened heart of a lonely night. Ling Nam as an institution was seen as threatening, even menacing to the cultural integrity of the country. The Pacific Academy instead was viewed as a social asset, another essential connection to his American benefactors. Given this approval, the school was very popular, students eager to speak "American English" flocking to its composition and conversation classes. How academically demanding and rigorous it was, I can't begin to say, given that many of the teachers were off-duty support personnel and diplomatic officials' wives. If not learned, at least trendy, blending official government doctrine, embattled Vietnamese culture, Chinese Roman Catholicism and America the Beautiful in one, big scholastic pot stirred by American cooks of somewhat questionable culinary background and skills.

Milton enjoyed his two years at the academy, the combination of a less rigid structure and friendlier teachers making for a pleasant environment, a description not normally ascribed to Ling Nam. This played favorably with him, further reinforcing his view of American superiority in comparison to what he had known. Because of his mother, he saw himself as more parts American than anything else. He wasn't Vietnamese and never could be. Ling Nam assured that. Of course he was Chinese, speaking both Cantonese and Mandarin but still, he had never lived in China, and wasn't planning on moving. America then was his great aspiration, and indeed inspiration, of who he could theoretically be and actually become. He felt his continued stay in Saigon to be temporary. It was well known that his mother had obtained American entrance visas for all of the children. With Rodney's departure, it was only logical that he and Michael would be next. Though his parents hadn't mentioned anything specific, it would seem to follow a natural and logical progression. This was more hopeful thinking than anything else. He needed some dream to grasp on to. In the meanwhile, he enjoyed his classes, working hard every day upon his English language fluency.

Soon after Rodney had left for Seattle, Wainam suddenly withdrew the twins from Father Louie's school, ordering them to remain confined at home. Milton swears he has no idea why this happened. They were doing perfectly well. They were happy. Now this abrupt, unexplained reversal in direction and course, taking them this way, then that way, upside down and inside out. Making it worse, nothing was said about any future plans concerning anything. Certainly nothing was said about Seattle.

They were now their father's prisoners, under house arrest for newer unknown crimes, forbidden to leave the flat.

One possible unstated reason for their abrupt withdrawal was Diem's rapid political deterioration, his popularity declining both in Washington, D.C., and amongst his own military officers. Wainam, in his role as a business negotiator, had to be aware of Diem's potential collapse. Perhaps it was merely seen as a good business tactic to create some distance between himself and any of Diem's associates. The unfortunate Diem and his brother, Ngo Dinh Nhu, were assassinated in a CIA-backed coup in 1963. The brothers were killed while their hands were tied behind their backs. The agreement had been to allow them to safely live in exile. This unfortunate brutality spoke volumes concerning the character of the South Vietnamese generals behind the Putsch, America's courageous and moral allies.

Anyway, whatever the reason, it was an irrational expectation to keep the twins confined to the flat. Finally their father had gone too far. And of course they were no longer children but young men, now 17 years old, wanting and needing far more than Wainam would ever allow. The simple solution was to have them join their siblings in Seattle, just getting rid of them, out of sight and out of mind. It's too obvious but somehow Wainam must have felt compelled to continue punishing them. I don't know what their mother thought, or whether she even knew what was happening, as it's unclear if she was still residing with her husband.

For Milton and Michael, it was the breaking point, the start of an open rebellion, finally freeing them from Wainam's dominance, no longer caring what his opinion was one way or the other. They became conspiratorial, trying to figure a way out. Describing them as merely angry doesn't match their fury. Nearly all their barriers had broken down to a kind of madness. Though never openly expressed, they hated their father for all of the many justifiable reasons, this current episode no more unreasonable than all the others. To hell with loyalty, feeling they owed him little or nothing, having been treated like trash blowing down Ky Con Street.

All of Wainam's control depended on the twins' adherence to an instilled Confucian code of ethics. Without their cooperation, he had none, depending upon an invisible and theoretical leash, the twins finally realizing he had no real physical hold upon them. The maids were not prison guards. They could and now would do whatever they wanted.

Of course not knowing what to do didn't help, but somehow they had to free themselves, escaping from their father's tyranny once and for all. There was no denying their father's attitude, viewing them as obstacles, something to be discarded, tossed away. It was insulting. It was intolerable to be treated like animals or worse. They were ready to strike back and hurt their father.

Wainam's love of language was genuine, something he intuitively responded to. Over the years he had accumulated a sizable and quite valuable book collection written in a variety of languages, including rare first editions. He certainly cared more about his books than he did for the twins, making his collection the perfect, undefended target. In a daring response to their father's intransigence, they began stealing his books right off the shelves and selling them, obviously not concerned about the consequences. And possibly even bolder, they raided his closets, actually selling their father's finely tailored business suits. What sweet revenge! With new-found change in their pockets, they were now wild in the streets, seeking out their friends in Saigon's countless cafes and pool halls. What a fun-filled spree it was, lasting all of one week, coming to an abrupt and sudden conclusion.

It could be said that Wainam was literally shocked into a reassessment, though unfortunately, not strongly enough to put the twins on the next airplane out of there. He was deeply wounded yet finally understanding that this time he was to blame.

Usually, his version of normal was to never take responsibility for anything, the blaming of others a fine art and life ambition.

Though this time his actions had gone too far, his underlying agenda now turned against himself. Simply punishing Milton and Michael was no longer sustainable. He also saw the potential that his private terror campaign could suddenly become very public. Some booksellers had already called him. However reluctantly, he would have to start acting like a father, not a prison warden, finally doing something positive. Instead of allowing the twins to run unfettered on the street, he found both of them jobs. It wasn't at all difficult because he was the one doing the hiring, becoming their first employer. It was all a matter of volition. With the twins he only did the minimum, what was necessary, and not much else.

In his position as a professional business negotiator, Wainam helped arrange housing for the thousands of American military advisors flooding into Saigon. He negotiated the renting of entire hotels for the incoming officers, arranging everything they could possibly need, the comforts of home away from home in a foreign land.

In addition to all that, he had become a subcontractor for the maid and laundry services, and it was there he installed the twins, now in charge of inspecting the rooms after they had been cleaned. It's not like they had much to do, falling in the category of busy work but certainly much better than stealing from their father. Their salary was 20,000 South Vietnamese piastre or dong, a month, then roughly equivalent to $20.00 in American currency. It wasn't much, even for a teenager. One major side benefit kind of made up for the low wages, for being the boss's son gave him and Michael instant celebrity, suddenly popular amongst the mostly female cleaning staff.

Milton and Michael worked in the hotels for nearly two years, it all being fairly mundane and boring except for the final nine months or so of their gainful employment, during which they added a little freelancing to their regular duties. As it turned out, placing the twins in the hotels was not dissimilar to putting foxes in with the hens. You could say that a few feathers flew, and still using poultry idioms, the twins suddenly flew the coop! The twins weren't bad kids, only abused and slightly feral, not understanding boundaries having known too many restrictions. When you don't know, you simply don't, the twins having no true idea where they were going, with no plan to take them there. If there was a wrong turn to be taken, they took it, stepping on the accelerator.

Three
American Advisors
& Chicanery in Saigon

B y mid 1962 the United States had placed more than 12,000 military advisors throughout South Vietnam, assisting with the broadening and modernization of its defense systems, and more hopefully, instructing the South Vietnamese army on how to fight a very unconventional adversary. It wasn't going to work.

Fidel Castro's Cuba was thumbing its nose at America, reminding all Americans from one coastline to the other that the Communist (with a capital C) menace was indeed real and actually preparing to turn everyone's little Johnny and Judy into Soviet-hugging automatons. The popular and ascendant attitude, circa the Joseph McCarthy era, was that if you give an inch, they will take the entire country.

Given this prevalent national fear, President Kennedy decided that faraway South Vietnam would be the appropriate place to display America's resolution, especially since Cuba then was essentially a Soviet Union satellite state, and to kick Cuba would be taken as punching the Russian bear. The Cuban missile crisis dramatically illustrated that now obvious point. Far safer to kick up some dust in some remote, seldom-remembered corner of the world than battering an island ninety miles south of Key West.

As I alluded to earlier, exaggerating threats is a time-honored American tradition. Any excuse will do. Demonize completely innocent Japanese-Americans, and intern them (Executive Order 9066), like FDR did in 1941. Most recently, the many justifications named by the Bush administration to invade Iraq, and when not discovering any weapons of mass destruction, etcetera, telling the American voters there were other equally good reasons for going to war. Hey Dick Cheney, for a Halliburton nickel or a dime, will deceive the American people and Congress anytime! No, specious reasoning and rationale was not confined to Kennedy and 1962, unfortunately appearing to be as popular now as in the not-too-distant past.

When does promotion end and propaganda begin? It's an all-important question when listening to governmental explanation. Is it the real information pertaining to a given issue or problem, or has it been somehow altered, or even worse, simply made up? It probably would have been helpful for the American voting public to have had such considerations during then-Vice President Lyndon Baines Johnson's glorified publicity tour of South Vietnam.

Designed to bolster South Vietnamese fighting spirit, hold the course and all that, it ended in a summit meeting with Diem, LBJ loftily comparing him with Great Britain's WW II-era prime minister, Winston Churchill, and England's finest hour, equating Nazi aggression with South Vietnam's more recent struggle. Given this kind of blatant rhetoric, it's surprising there weren't a few RAF Spitfires and Hurricanes winging over the podium. I wonder if LBJ knew that many of Ho Chi Mihn's fundamental principals were based on the American constitution, possibly learned when he was washing dishes and shoveling snow in New York City, one of his many stops during his years of worldwide travel.

What LBJ failed to convey and fully articulate to Diem was that the Western governments viewed his beloved South Vietnam as a sacrificial lamb, a grand political experiment leading to the proverbial slaughterhouse, not mattering to them if the laboratory burst into flames, frying all involved. Like any good salesman, LBJ was there to sell a policy. He was there to stop Communism, and to hell with the fine print, the Kennedy administration either failing or not caring to consult the history books and turning to all the pages concerning interference in a nation's internal affairs.

Sadly, all they really needed to do was read about their own American revolution to be reminded that people truly resent being meddled with, not liking to be told what is supposedly good for them—just take this bitter medicine and unfair taxation and everything will be fine in the morning. Their mistake was basic, forgetting their own roots, like the pigs in George Orwell's *Animal Farm*, once smart, clear-thinking animals now transformed into greedy, old farmers. The United States was proceeding headlong into disaster, slamming into an immovable wall. Despite using more explosive power than was dropped during WW II, including the atomic attacks on Hiroshima and Nagasaki, they were unable to blow up or knock that wall down.

An interesting side note is that many American generals, including the notorious Curtis LeMay, who was George Wallace's vice-presidential running mate in 1968, advocated more than once the use of tactical nuclear weapons against the North Vietnamese. Can you imagine what our world would look like if that door had been reopened? Is this what the so-called "best and the brightest" had to offer as coherent foreign policy? Another footnote is the current attitude of the average American. In an anniversary poll of the nuclear bombings conducted in 2009, over seventy percent of the American public believes that the attacks were justified but that doesn't appear to stop any of them from driving a Toyota or Honda. No, no, don't take my Lexus away!

From the very beginning, the United States was contradictory, not truly having a robust appetite for a real war, just a quick intervention, a brief fling, not a prolonged engagement resulting in a serious martial marriage. I have never taken seriously the contention that the Vietcong and North Vietnamese won the war. That is an erroneous assessment.

The reality beyond any other myth is that America withdrew because of the opposition's staying power, displaying an almost suicidal resolve, a willingness to sacrifice every man, woman and child. How do you defeat that? They proved a relentless opponent, knock them down and up they popped back, swinging. No matter how many bombs dropped and hundreds of thousands killed, the Viet Cong and the North Vietnamese relentlessly refused to give up, "surrender" not part of their ideological vocabulary, alien to their natural instincts.

Of course the United States held the ability to win decisively: the manpower, the leadership, the technology, the economic, owning every poker chip save one, which was the will, the determination for winning at any cost, a price probably translating into, who knows, maybe two hundred thousand additional American deaths or more, meaning an unflinching land invasion of North Vietnam. If an invasion had occurred, my guess is that it would have become known as possibly the bloodiest conflict the modern world had ever witnessed, making the current conflicts in Iraq and Afghanistan look like pleasant strolls through a park on a Saturday afternoon.

As it was, the weekly casualties were nonetheless appalling. Anyone of near adult age in the late 1960s will never forget the shocking Vietnam War death tallies, local and national newspapers listing the names of the hundreds of mostly conscripted young men (a sizable percentage minority) dying weekly, incomprehension rivaling the implausible while the public kept count of the unfortunate dead, blatantly obvious to the Johnson and then Nixon administrations that the American voting public would never tolerate nor accept a ground invasion.

You could get away with invading Cambodia but not North Vietnam. The folk-rock group Country Joe & the Fish sang something about you being lucky enough to be the first one on your block to have your son return home in a box. All crass humor and sarcasm aside, the war and its impact on Vietnam and the United States really wasn't humorous, no levity to be found in a tear-stained cemetery.

Though back in 1962, the earliest stages of the conflict still held some degree of innocence to some oblivious minds, Saigon somehow a weekend jaunt to the local country club, nothing more. Lending to that misconception were the hotel accommodations, the "Bachelor Officer Quarters", or BOQs, as they were better known, that the military advisors were assigned to, rows of gigantic luxury hotels, looming privileged edifices ruling over Saigon's waterfront and teeming streets. The BOQs, as designed, were self-contained worlds, providing everything, within practical limits, the officers might need and desire after a hard day in the steaming jungle. They were a refuge, a place to forget about the war for a few hours, and get your clothes laundered and pressed too.

It was in this setting that the twins found themselves, rotating between four BOQs, all within a five-block radius. All day up and down, floor to floor Milton would travel, each and every elevator having its own personality. His duties were fairly limited. Carrying out the dirty laundry and inspecting all the maid's handiwork was the prevailing daily theme. He was bored. You might guess there's only so much novelty in a hotel room, pretty soon each and every one the same, clean or dirty making little difference to the staid observer. While pleased to be doing something, anything, Milton remained far from satisfied, a disembodied spirit floating down the hallways, upset and angry with his father, with fate, with himself, locked in an internal argument that he couldn't escape. Emotionally, Milton had remained essentially the same, still relatively young, never knowing what next to do. This small authority over the fate of bedrooms had barely altered him, knowing as much as he had been taught. Ling Nam ultimately hadn't been the best of teachers, failing to inform him of the big, wide world just waiting to swallow him up.

Milton's personal contact with the American officers was normally fairly peripheral. In most cases he was unable to connect individual names and faces. Really, for Milton, they seemed to have appeared from another world, one not quite real, not men but almost mythical beings descended down from some remote mountaintop, an abode of the imagined Gods. His yearning for the United States had turned into a kind of new religiosity, Seattle his version of Mecca, the capital of his holy land, the spiritual home he never had. America now came to represent everything good, while South Vietnam, his actual home, symbolized everything bad and disabling. This same emotion motivated him to contact the kind of Americans he could easily reach out to: the thousands of enlisted support personnel that were typing forms, driving jeeps, guarding the BOQs. Not quite deities but divine enough to suit Milton, his cosmology not all that complicated.

Now with just a little bit of change in his pockets, Milton started exploring Saigon's neighborhoods and entertainments, inching ever closer to actually touching what was once thought unattainable: the sometimes sordid amusements of a city in the midst of war. This led him to become an unofficial guide to equally green young American lads touring the more seamy sides of Saigon, the thousands of bars and nightclubs filled with enticing Vietnamese and Cambodian girls all waiting to sit on your lap, "and please, Mister Soldier Boy, I would like another drink (Giggle! Giggle!)" Milton's payment was usually a few drinks and a front row seat for all the ongoing craziness. Finally in his short, long life he was enjoying himself, inhaling freedom as well as the cigarette smoke-laden air.

Milton, quite accidentally it appears, had learned a valuable survival skill, which was to be likeable, to be instantly friendly with everyone he met. All those years and countless moments avoiding his father's wrath taught him how to be inoffensive, when to be compliant. If Wainam was a professional middleman, his son was now a professional pal, one of the guys, laughing at all the jokes good and bad. Learned out of self-preservation, this kind of deprecation would one day pay off handsomely, with no one wanting to see Milton hurt, thereby protecting and shielding him from potentially bad outcomes.

During his future stint in the United States Army, he would attract a series of human guardian angels guiding him through trouble, Milton uncannily remaining unscathed. To his credit, out of an extreme deficit, Milton created a positive surplus, a protective aura shielding him from the worst circumstances.

Milton made one good friend out of the varied assortment of newly arrived serviceman, Jim, an Army Specialist Four hailing from Chicago, Illinois. Milton met Jim at a very singular event, both witnessing an old Vietnamese Buddhist priest, Thich Quang Duc, lighting himself on fire, the first in a dramatic series of self-immolations that would take place all across South Vietnam, fiery protests against the expanding war and a corrupt government. Call it a bonding experience. Jim was shocked beyond his Midwestern comprehension, even for a city kid—the monk's saffron robes a sudden appalling ball of smoke and leaping flames.

Later, Jim would become well acquainted with both Milton and Michael, becoming a kind of surrogate big brother, treating them as equals, for unlike so many other South Vietnamese, they weren't trying to manipulate him into or out of anything. Also a number of months later, he would provide an invaluable service, transporting some of the twins' ill-gotten gains once they had reached Hong Kong. I have wondered if he ever knew the true source of all those dollar bills, as Jim, contrary to too many bad examples, epitomized the best of American intentions. There were many who truly believed in the moral integrity of the American intervention, united in a common cause against evil, who were prepared, like the aforementioned Buddhist monk, to offer the ultimate sacrifice. While it may be true that some people can be convinced concerning the efficacy of nearly anything, unvarnished idealism did exist in the hearts of many of those involved. Jim, like so many unknown others, simply tried to make the best of a truly untenable and insane situation.

As Jim himself discovered, an avaricious, rapacious environment greeted the American liberators, temporary madness engulfing the population, too many years of being without hope now toppling all reason and common sense—money, the making of money replacing all other rational considerations. Saigon was now no longer a Vietnamese city. Instead it was an instant American theme park called the "Land of Ultimate Opportunity," a carnival-filled atmosphere that offered the usually unobtainable for almost fair-market prices. An American couldn't walk down the streets without being bombarded by offers and enticements promising you heaven twenty-four hours a day, including Sundays. Who needed a church, or a separate Sabbath day when you carried this new theology with you, an insular and selfish creed sheltered by a celestial sky raining American dollars. Into this fertile greenback fantasyland stepped the twins, intoxicated by the fragrant incense and elaborate ceremony, serenaded by fervent choirs in full voice. Filled with pious rapture, Milton too lifted up his arms, praying skyward seeking sweet blessings, untold blessings, vowing to be forever faithful to a God most good and kind.

And who says prayers are never answered? Don't believe it. Milton's certainly were, a priest soon thereafter arriving at their door beckoning, describing the wonders of an unseen world made manifest. In other words he informed them how they could make some quick and easy money, "No risk! No problems! So come on, why not sign up now and try today, your pockets instantly filling with cash!" Who the heck could resist that kind of offer? Why it would be positively un-American, especially for two youngsters striving to be as American as possible while living half a world away from those golden shores.

What really happened was that an old neighbor came knocking: Mister Ding, sole proprietor of the local welding shop. Ding had obviously acquired a new prosperity, his usual soiled coveralls and heavy work boots now replaced by a far more congenial outfit consisting of a clean white shirt, neatly pressed khaki trousers and polished black shoes.

Now here he was, Ding the welder, standing smiling at the flat's threshold looking more like an American Mormon missionary than the better known rough and ready laborer. And not only well-dressed, the once sweaty welder had also recently joined the motorized age, now represented by a brand new, bright red motor scooter, Ding's smile nearly as sparkling as his scooter glinting in the tropical sun. Circumstances had definitely changed for Ding, and that's why he had come, wanting to know if the twins were interested in doing a little business involving all those rich American army officers. He had a proposal, some simple transactions that were guaranteed to make everyone concerned happy and contented.

It was common knowledge, the subject of neighborhood gossip; that the twins were now working for their father at the BOQs. The prevalent assumption was that the twins had remained behind in Saigon because they were in line to take over their father's varied business interests. The gossips surmised that after three years, like Wainam, they too had developed their own personal set of contacts, self-interest an inherited trait. For them, Milton and Michael's future was preordained, just a matter of time, and because of that, the twins were just another Saigon commodity to exploit, however benignly. To Ding's way of thinking, this was more than just making a personal profit. The twins would be providing a kind of public service, spreading the wealth far and wide.

Whether this was all clear to the twins, it certainly was to

Ding, who knew a good situation when he saw it. To Ding it was all just simple addition, adding one contact to the next creating one larger sum that would then be divided equally from the total. What could be easier, more simple and straight-forward than that, not at all complicated, just like Ding. Life was good, so why not share some of its bounty with his neighbors?

Ding's proposition was as basic as he was. He now represented an international syndicate, a group of discreet businessmen interested in obtaining as many American dollars as they could, the dollar of course being the most viable currency. If they wanted to, they could ask their American officer friends if they would like to do some monetary exchanges at very favorable rates. You bring me the dollars in cash, checks or money orders, Ding not caring. In return I will flood you with more piastres than you have ever seen, with the understanding of course that you will give yourselves a small handling fee for all your trouble. How does that sound? And I'm always available, any time, any place. Here's my telephone number. See you around!

After delivering his practiced sales pitch, Ding zipped away on his scooter, a very busy man, leaving the twins both impressed and utterly shocked. What had he just offered them? Was it legal? It all seemed suspicious—but of course that didn't mean it didn't hold possibilities. The major hurdle was no one they knew had any money, not in the quantities Ding was seeking. Jim and his soldier friends certainly didn't. As to all their big officer friends they didn't know any. In fact, they were scared of them. So what to do, what to do?

With Ding's offer of 20 to 30 piastre per dollar over the official exchange rates, there had to be a solution. It was too good to pass up. Ding knew that, knowing well his potential clientele and how greed is contagious. They understood this could literally be their ticket to Seattle. It had been three years since Rodney had left and still not one mention of Seattle. They were now completely convinced that they would never get out if it was left to their father. There had to be a way to do this. As it turned out, the answer was obvious, sitting out in open view. All they had to do was reach for it. It was that simple.

The American officers, you might say rather naively, viewed the BOQs as their homes, a much needed sanctuary from ambushes and bullets. Who needed to think about threats when all they wanted to do was relax, throw off the muddy boots and sit down, with no concerns furrowing their brows? Just like back in their real home in the States, they naturally put everything anywhere--- wallets, watches, checkbooks. You name the item, you would find it strewn here and there upon the bed stands and tables and desks, having no good reason to distrust the maids or anyone else concerning this particular matter. At least that's what they thought. Once they passed the entryway and saluted the guards they were through with looking over their shoulder. The day was done, now time for a Jack Daniels on the rocks. To hell with it all!

The twins' job was to be observant. Was the toilet bowl clean? Did the maids put out fresh towels? Were the officers personal items left undisturbed? This is what Milton did on his daily rounds, his tidy patrol, making sure everything was okay and taking pride that finally his father couldn't discover any faults. His initial attitude was correct, that the officers' personal belongings were inviolate, not to be touched, but unfortunately, opportunity met desperation, resulting in an unexpected deviation, the temptation being too great. Milton and Michael came up with a novel idea. If the officers wouldn't write checks to Ding, then instead they would have to write them. There was nothing else to do.

Their idea was reasonably clever. Instead of causing an alarm by stealing an entire checkbook, they instead would very carefully tear a check from the center, hoping beyond hope that it would go unnoticed, each time selecting a different victim. They never had a problem finding a legible signature to copy from. Besides,

Ding couldn't speak or read a single word of English, so they didn't expect any protests from him.

Their plan was simple, and much wiser—if they had only followed their own advice. The thought was to write a few checks, saving all the money and get out of town before the checks started bouncing, somehow thereafter making their way to Seattle. Being more mature, that's exactly what they would have done, but being themselves, they were going to make it difficult. Milton and Michael were about ready to become slightly more than petty criminals, so I suppose it made sense to be irresponsible as well as dishonest, living the role, just not acting it out. Success was alien. Failure, that old and familiar friend, was always close by, willing and able to be of assistance.

Amazingly, without asking any questions, Ding happily took the checks, more than pleased, elated. One can only imagine his percentage, his cut of this type of transaction. He certainly wasn't doing any of this for free. Whoever his backers were, they must have had tremendous resources, for in their initial enthusiasm, the twins' two checks totaled ten thousand dollars. Nothing like starting modestly, taking one small step after the other. It really doesn't seem possible for this to have occurred. Though sounding like bad fiction, Milton swears it did, both on this particular day and various other numerous occasions.

True to his word, Ding returned carrying a satchel containing more money than Milton thought possible. It was completely crazy, not making any sense whatsoever. The explanation though was simple. It was wartime Saigon at its best, or taking the reverse perspective, its worst.

Milton and Michael were stunned, dazed, physically and emotionally overwhelmed by the bundles of piastres now in their possession. It was unbelievable but true. Instantaneously they had become a walking, talking bank vault, but of course minus the usual security.

Truth be told, they had never actually believed their scheme would succeed. Now that it had, they didn't now know what to do. Though having talked about leaving, no definite plans had been made. Instead of this clarifying their situation, it became all the more confusing. Now having the means to move forward, they were stuck in an internal morass of their own making. Since everything was bad, nothing was good enough.

What they were confronted with was something essential to their situation. The problem, at least new to them, was that they didn't understand themselves or the potential freedom this shady deal had provided them. It was going to take a few months to comprehend their new reality. But as the saying goes, time waits for no one, the twins certainly receiving no exemption. Events would overtake them, whether they were prepared or not. They were up to their necks and the water was rising. And they had never bothered to take swimming lessons.

This sudden wealth uncovered an unacknowledged truth. Despite having all their hopes and dreams pinned on Seattle, the concept and ideal of Seattle, the city was in reality only symbolic of a life desired and dreamt, the locale essentially unimportant. What truly mattered most of all was finally feeling alive, of making decisions that counted for something, feeling connected and not severed from humanity itself.

This is how they felt, how they were, half-crazy from a lifetime of being told they were little better than nothing. Their true salvation lay not in locale but in rejecting their father's abuse, not giving it legitimacy. Looking in the mirror they saw that they were breathing, not dead nor buried but standing upright, with the will and a genuine right to live a full and long life.

Remaining in Saigon would have been fine had they felt a good cause to stay, but that was part of their tragedy, their early life theme being somewhere but nowhere at all. Human beings are not ghosts, floating on the edge of existence, but flesh and blood bonded to the earth, requiring and expecting human recognition and embrace, anchoring them physically and cognitively to all they know and love. It wasn't Seattle they wanted. That faraway city tucked away in the northwest corner of the United States had nothing to do with it.

What the twins needed once and for all was to be somewhere, anywhere—to be wanted and seen and most of all, appreciated. They didn't know how to get what they needed but that wouldn't delay them. Regardless of the destination, be it Seattle or Hong Kong or a shallow grave, that's where they were going, having taken no for an answer too many times to stop now,

By cashing those first checks, they set in motion a series of mostly inevitable and unavoidable circumstances, taken by the shirt collar and pulled relentlessly down that road, an irreversible decision leading to complete and utter change.

Again, by accepting Ding's offer, they had descended down to a personal perdition, now at least temporarily criminal, subject to a new and very different set of laws and codes, a world both extremely dangerous and potentially fatal. It was just like the twins to blindly sell their souls to the devil, then blithely shake hands over the deal, not remembering their Ling Nam Bible studies, when Satan set Jesus upon a mountain top, offering him the world—but for a price, only for a small, non-negotiable price.

Meanwhile, their friend, the ever-benevolent Ding, still thinking everything was fine, the usual honor amongst thieves, pressured Milton for more checks. Already uncomfortable, Milton became hesitant, actually telling Ding that he couldn't guarantee the checks, but Ding remained adamant, reassuring that there were no problems, having nothing to worry about.

If only that had been anything remotely close to the truth. Did Ding ever think to ask himself just why the Americans would need that much South Vietnamese currency? I suppose old-fashioned greed colored his better judgment—money, especially easy money, notorious for such lapses. For the twins, this was all unrehearsed theatrics. For Ding it was just business as usual. All this notwithstanding, within a few months the twins had passed over $50,000 in bogus checks, not bad work, obviously easier than anything they had ever done. But even Milton understood that this situation couldn't continue. They would be murdered if they didn't depart the country without delay.

A growing uneasiness concerning the ultimate wisdom of their dubious actions finally prompted some mature decision making. Needing some kind of official identification to legally and openly leave the country, they formally applied for their national identity cards at the Saigon National Police station. That this also exposed them to potential conscription into the Army of the Republic Of Vietnam, better known by the initials ARVN, was now a small secondary concern versus the very real probability of being executed by some self-styled mafia for "non-payment of funds." Enduring three days of long lines, interminable waits, and bored, governmental indifference definitely seemed the better alternative.

They weren't the only ones, however, interested in leaving. Impending disaster lingered in the general atmosphere, hovering above Saigon, an unpredictable political weather front—puffy, ominous clouds weighting upon the populace. This particular misery could have been avoided, if like their siblings, IDs had been obtained by the parents in the first place.

The sad sequel to all this is that the police station, along with the twins' pending applications, were destroyed in a Vietcong attack, a massive fire consuming both the building and their last initiative for a legal departure. It didn't take much to undermine them. The thought of renewing the process was just too daunting, meaning in their minds it was time to flee the country, to just get out of town.

Throughout this period of newfound wealth and profound indecision, Milton and Michael had been busily introducing themselves to a new lifestyle fueled by the forgeries. Instead of saving money, they spent it as quickly as it arrived, indulging in all the obvious physical pleasures.

And now in addition to working in hotels, Milton lived in them, having been effectively barred from the flat, Wainam not at pleased with the twins' behavior, at times crossing paths with his sons while pursuing his own questionable agenda. At this point, Milton had reached the pinnacle of his defiance, no disguising his derision and open disdain. The money had changed everything, providing him with new permissions, a different subtext for living.

Also adding to this new confidence was his first relationship, having recently met Fong, a young, married waitress working at a favorite restaurant. Yes, life was going well. He certainly didn't need his meddling father to tell him how to live.

Unfortunately, what goes up sometimes comes down, an abrupt descent to obvious reality. In August, nearly eight months after the first forgery, a check was returned for non-payment. It appears Ding's friends were using some unusual methods or financial avenues to process the checks. If the twins had been wise, they would have been gone weeks ago. Amazingly, Ding pressured them for another check. If Ding didn't understand what was happening, they certainly did. A terminus had been reached and they were at the end of the line. Their wild ride was nearly over.

Their first response badly backfired, having decided to confide to some of their hoodlum buddies, handing over a few thousand dollars, thinking there would be safety in numbers. Instead these would-be protectors turned on the twins, essentially blackmailing them, threatening to tell Ding all about it, but it appears that was hardly necessary.

September brought more returned checks and an abrupt change in Ding's demeanor. No longer was he the completely trusting neighbor. Still, with the evidence staring at him, Ding remained reasonable, not fully grasping the extent of the twins' treachery, holding to the very thin belief that everything was okay. It probably hadn't occurred to him that his secret friends might ultimately hold him responsible. Ding remained the local welder, criminal activity for him only a part-time hobby.

October's arrival brought more bouncing checks and an increased agitation. Ding was now visibly unhappy. It was time to say goodbye to Saigon. Only one question remained to be answered. Was there anyone left in the entire city that they could trust to get them out? And very lucky for them, there was one such rare individual who was willing to help, for a price of course but nonetheless prepared to assist these wayward souls toward any destination they wished, doing his best to get them there, never questioning his client's hearts or motivations, knowing that others would do that for him.

Four

Escape: Phnom Penh & Cows Bound For Hong Kong

Tall Tong was a well-known family friend, a sometimes visitor to Number 24, certainly a local neighborhood character, having earned the reputation as a smooth operator, maybe best described as an alternative "jack of all trades," especially the slightly nefarious ones. Knowing nearly everybody worth knowing for making an unimpeded dollar, Tall Tong was a master of the quick and easy connection, obviously similar to Wainam but more worldly in his operations.

Depending on your needs, Tall Tong was indispensable, his knowledge as towering as he was, over six feet and straight and slender as a human chopstick. If he couldn't swing or finagle a deal himself, he always knew someone who could, his referral of course coming with a small handling fee but what was money when you urgently required a difficult and discreet service, and besides, all his recommendations came with a personal guarantee. No worries. Tall Tong would never fail you, your troubles now his concern.

The twins' problem was not unique. You needed to get out of the country quickly, like pronto, well fine, no problem, Tall Tong would be your travel agent. Now the means of transport might be slightly unusual, but again, aren't surprises one of the

51

hidden charms of traveling to distant and unknown places? Why, uncertainty just made the adventure more thrilling, just a little more thankful when you arrived safely and intact. Though viewing it quite accurately, did you really have any other choice?

Obviously now, Milton and Michael were beyond all options save an immediate departure, and quickly please, before Ding's invisible partners suddenly materialized, wasting no time avenging their substantial debt. They also feared their father's reaction if Ding approached Wainam, but figured quite correctly how unlikely that was, Ding afraid of having to explain how he got the twins involved in all this nonsense. If Wainam ever knew of their big secret, he never told them. At the brink of their own disaster, at their wit's end, trusting no one, they knew they had to believe that Tall Tong remained their friend despite anything he might have suspected.

If he did know their story, he never let on, always treating them with his usual courtesy and kindness, remaining totally frank and honest, which considering the underworld he inhabited, spoke volumes. The twins never understood the risk Tall Tong himself was taking, knowing that Wainam would not appreciate any meddling with his own family. Though Tall Tong certainly must have thought it odd what Milton and Michael were doing, especially given their family's standing in the community, he never mentioned it. Of course, ever the professional, he remained discreet. He saw all the other children fly away. It was obvious something was seriously amiss, though given the many titles he held; social worker just couldn't be one of them.

Amazingly, the twins' pot of gold had dwindled down to around ten thousand dollars, or about twenty percent of what they had originally stolen. Talk about flushing a small fortune down a silver-plated toilet. Tall Tong, who could have literally requested anything, told them that for two thousand dollars, payable immediately, he would get them to Hong Kong. From there they would be on their own. It was that simple, giving them a date exactly two weeks from their conversation, telling them to stand on a particular corner, where a car would stop and take them away. Just be ready, Tall Tong said, and have a nice trip.

Taking their money—that was the last they ever saw of him. Maybe he just didn't want to be around and witness any accidents. All he could guarantee was his small part of the agreement, it being up to them to remain alive and keep their appointment. The thing Tall Tong didn't want to do was face Wainam after some unforeseen event. Wainam had powerful connections. Tall Tong never liked complications. Too messy! Tall Tong was only interested in certainties, dodging at all costs the lower percentages.

Two weeks were never longer, seconds and minutes clinging to Milton like perspiration, blurring his vision, the unknown weighting his steps. Hours were now dangerous obstacles. Nightfall became an encircling wall. Milton was justifiably terrified, afraid of moving forward or standing still, the ensuing two weeks disorienting and threatening. Every stranger became a potential assassin, with every moment becoming his last. Even friends were suspect, someone to be avoided. His fear even prevented him from telling Fong, promising himself he would write once he reached Seattle.

His life was now unreal. Milton starred in his own movie as the irretrievable lost soul condemned to mutely strolling eternally darkened streets, every sound and noise of course whispering impending doom. And suddenly he was religious, fearing God's wrath and retribution, remembering that looming Jesus residing over Ling Nam. Milton though needn't have worried, at that point errant Chinese Baptists a low priority—not with so many misbehaving Buddhists to attend to, burning themselves to a cinder, trying to gain God's attention as if God wasn't already seriously preoccupied with the ongoing war and other assorted problems of the livelong day.

Despite all fears to the contrary, Milton and Michael were not run over by a speeding truck or required to wear cement galoshes. Nothing happened at all except their usual and mundane confusion, a continuing routine of well-trodden endless circles ultimately leading back to the beginning.

Again, nothing changed, no great conclusions reached or decisions made. No additional preparations either, other than entrusting their American comrade, Jim, with the majority of their money to be personally delivered at some unknown future date in Hong Kong. At least they thought they would make it that far. They certainly hoped to.

Finally, the fateful day arrived, and true to Tall Tong's word, a sedan pulled up at the appointed corner and hour, the driver wordlessly motioning them to enter. So standing there, minus luggage or jackets, literally with only the shirts upon their backs, they embarked on the most important journey of their young lives, their initial destinations all question marks along an unknown highway. Their uninterested chauffeur, taciturn and sullen, barely uttered a word as he turned south out of Saigon, obviously heading in the direction of the greater Mekong River delta. For better, or quite possibly worse, the twins were finally on their way to Seattle.

One hour, two hours they rode, trading the pavement for dusty, winding roads taking them ever further from the city, and deeper, always deeper into the thick jungle canopy, lush growth brushing, scratching the car's sides, an irritating, banging chorus of metallic shrieks and whines. No one spoke, the twins not knowing what to think or feel, easier to just quietly sit. Milton didn't want to be doing this but here he was, now totally subject to fate's whim and fancy, a prisoner uncertain of parole. He simply had no response to what was happening to him. Everything felt mechanical, without human volition, Milton a speechless automaton blankly staring ahead, seeing and feeling nothing at all.

Without warning, the driver slammed to an abrupt stop,

jerking the twins out of their stupor, and without any kind of explanation, motioned that it was time to leave, the first leg of their journey obviously completed. With that they were unceremoniously kicked out, the driver roaring off, abandoning the forlorn pair to whatever the situation brought. Numb, too shocked to do anything but stare at the surrounding jungle, a friendly face suddenly appeared. It was an old Vietnamese fisherman who told them that he was to be their guide up the Mekong River and into Cambodia.

Leading them down a path near the river's edge they reached his green, thatched house where they later shared a delicious meal of rice and crab with the fisherman's family. Noting their youth, the fisherman kindly reassured them that everything was fine, that they were only two of many guests that he had successfully shepherded up the Mekong to safety. Milton finally relaxed a little, pleased with the fisherman, allowing himself some hope that he and Michael would actually make it to Hong Kong. Tall Tong had kept his word.

The river that the twins would soon be setting off upon, the mighty Mekong, has traditionally served as a watery highway heading upriver into Cambodia, eventually forming the Laos-Thailand border, continuing ever northward to its Tibetan headwaters.

A few centuries ago, French explorers searched the Mekong's furthest reaches in hopes of discovering a new trading route into China. Unfortunately their journey upriver was stymied by swift rapids and other navigational obstacles, the northern lengths unsuitable for large commercial vessels and traffic, though the southern waters exactly the opposite, perfect for the tramp steamer that would eventually take the twins from Phnom Penh into the South China Sea and on, and yes, you guessed it, to the British Crown Colony of Hong Kong.

As day became night, it was clear, clear as that big, iridescent full moon bathing the Mekong's black reflective surface with a soft illuminating light, that Tall Tong should have consulted a calendar before choosing this particular evening for the twins' departure. There would be no blanketing darkness this night, the moon a cheerful but most unwelcome beacon.

Nonetheless, the fisherman's canoe and its anxious cargo slipped noiselessly into the Mekong, Milton and Michael holding on tight, gazing up at the huge, white moon. The canoe, propelled by both motor and sail, glided quickly and purposefully toward the heavily shadowed opposite shoreline, quietly avoiding a South Vietnamese patrol craft traveling just northward, scanning the river with an intrusive searchlight. Deadening the engine and setting sail, they proceeded north hugging the foliage-draped shoreline, a muscular breeze steadily pushing them forward.

Milton, seated at the canoe's stern, staring up and around at the immensity of life surrounding him—the black, star-filled sky, the sweeping river, the dark impenetrable jungle—found himself overwhelmed by a lifelong grief and a recognition of failure, quietly sobbing, having had enough of this day, of his crazy existence, never feeling more isolated and alone. All he had were questions.

"How could this be happening? What have I done to deserve this?" he moaned into the night. Unfortunately Milton would not receive an answer as the wind-filled sail billowed above him, taking him to where he really didn't know, having never taken a minute to actually study a map of their prospective journey, now understanding that he was totally dependent upon chance and Tall Tong's unknown arrangements. This was no way to live. He knew that he couldn't continue like this. If the canoe suddenly capsized and they all drowned, sinking to the river bottom, who would know or care? It was completely unacceptable. Something had to change.

Though seeming a small eternity, the journey northward into Cambodian waters realistically took only eight to ten hours, the fisherman finally beaching his sturdy canoe upon a shady clearing, a mere shallow indentation pressed into the dense foliage. Early morning sunlight vainly struggled, searching for gaps and avenues between the tangled fraternization of glistening leaves and branches, the jungle awakening with the screeching song of an invisible multitude of hungry birds. Whispering he would be back soon, the fisherman disappeared, swallowed by a swaying sea of bamboo, leaving the twins alone to their own fearful comprehension, gripping the rough sides of the canoe as if it was their last material link to cultivated civilization, imaging venomous snakes and fearsome tigers and other biting things.

He was soon back but unfortunately with some very unpleasant news. Their next contact, a Cambodian farmer, had recently died from a sudden illness, and if it was possible, making their situation all the direr, the grief-stricken daughter had promptly fled the village, taking with her the knowledge of all their future arrangements and contacts—a link in Tall Tong's chain now irrevocably broken.

The fisherman, faithful to his task, reassured them that if no solution was found they were welcome to sail back with him. Milton was dumbfounded. To have come this far only to return was unthinkable. Milton and Michael could only blankly look at each other. There was nothing to say as it had already been spoken.

While the twins were mentally digesting this unexpected development, two young men emerged from the jungle, explaining that they knew where the two Vietnamese were to be taken, being friends of the farmer's family, and for a fee, would take them there. Of course who knew if they were telling the truth, but given the alternative, the twins negotiated payment, the Cambodian youths gladly accepting Milton's Rolex watch in return for a ride to Phnom Penh.

Happy with their new watch, probably worth a small fortune, they promptly took Milton and Michael aboard their motor scooters into the Cambodian capital, and amazingly, directly to the home of a Chinese family who had been awaiting their arrival.

Call it dumb luck, divine intervention, or just Tall Tong's guaranteed efficiency, all they had to do now was to wait for the freighter's captain to send word when it was time to come aboard. Now it was time to be patient and relax, feeling that they had just survived the most harrowing part of their odyssey, which, depending upon the point of view, was both true and false.

Despite their carnal rampage in Saigon, the twins remained innocents, far less worldly than their initial chaperon the old fisherman. Not just lacking vision, they lacked imagination, that vital ingredient merging the possible and impossible into tangible reality, allowing insight beyond the blatantly obvious.

The twins brief hiatus in Phnom Penh unexpectedly extended into an over two-week stay, unfortunately generating some unwanted friction. Their hosts, though kindly people, nervous harboring two obvious foreigners for so long, began to fear detection and arrest. Afraid to go, yet afraid to stay, the twins just sat there mutely day after day in a corner of the cramped apartment, waiting for this ordeal too to pass peacefully away without serious incident. Boredom and anxiety, not excitement, remained the prevalent theme. Finally, when word arrived that it was time to go, Milton looked forward to just walking and breathing fresh air as much as anything else, the commonplace suddenly an unexpected pleasure.

Their new guide, this time a dark-skinned, sun-baked sailor led the twins through the swerving mass that populated Phnom Penh's streets, winding this way and that down to the riverside docks, arriving at a scarred, rusting veteran of many watery travails. This mighty hulk, name and colors unknown, was floating there at wharf side building up steam for yet another voyage—huge, grayish, cloudy plumes wafting from a still vertical stack. The ship, this vessel the twins were about to board was your classic tramp steamer, truly a nautical museum piece, a weaver of tales and legends written upon salty pages—that day transformed into a more modern Noah's ark, transporting, sadly, not a magical and paired menagerie but a bawling, mooing herd of desperate cattle dancing a bovine jig of stamping hooves and sweaty haunches.

The steamer, though certainly not pretty, held a certain battered charm, innumerable voyages over at least seven seas etched and lined every inch of a pugnacious hull, her sharply angled bow proudly symbolizing a cutting defiance. Though weathered and bent, decades past her first youthful frolics, she remained seaworthy, more than prepared to transport the twins and the complaining cows and anything else to Hong Kong and ports beyond.

Once aboard, they were warmly greeted by the captain, an old Chinese salt bearing a face as weathered as his steamer's bow, cutting a line through all obvious pretensions. Recognizing the twins' anxiety, he put them at ease by saying they were already nearly in Hong Kong, just relax and enjoy the voyage. They were berthed with three other young, male castaways, a cabin maybe not commodious but at least dry, with only a few resident cockroaches, the door shutting tightly, barring the ocean spray and even the most adventurous of the ship's numerous seafaring rats.

The five-day sailing to Hong Kong was routinely uneventful, the normally moody elements cooperating the entire way, the steamer gently slicing through the smooth waters of the Mekong and then the South China Sea. The only perilous moments occurred while the ship was clearing South Vietnamese customs. Hidden deep within the hold were the five castaways, quickly diminishing their precious oxygen supply by unwisely smoking cigarettes, nearly resulting in their collective suffocation. After being held nearly six hours, the steamer suddenly lurched forward, thankfully sparing the captain from the unsolicited task of burying five wayward youths at sea. After that calamitous near miss, the twins made a point of getting lots of fresh air while watching the waves pass by, as much as possible avoiding serious thought and conversation.

Part of the documentation necessary to enter a foreign land.

Milton, far left, & Michael, second from right, well-dressed in Hong Kong.

Five
Hong Kong: Auntie Wong & Anyway, Just Where Is Jun Sung Park?

Hong Kong holds a unique position in fairly recent Asian history, being not only a great city and port, a celebrated gateway to every corner of the world, but also an unforeseen cultural melting pot, mixing Victorian British and dynastic Chinese civilization into a peculiarly endemic recipe: frumpy English tea and crumpets alongside mysterious restaurants featuring your favorite species of venomous snake, stir fried or steamed, your choice. Wrenched away from China by the British in the nineteenth century, it became, and remains, despite its recent return to the People's Republic, literally an island of stability set in the middle of a bubbling, tumultuous cauldron, lowering the temperature of anyone entering its oddly secular political and cultural environment.

Politically, our world in late 1963 was a very different place, far more stratified than what we know currently: a world divided into defensive armed camps glaring across broad ideological schisms, just daring one or the other to make a wrong move. It was a time when a claim of political oppression still held real legitimacy. To be a political refugee was a position that held respect, something to be assisted and aided. Not as it is too frequently today, with immigrants instantly labeled social pariahs, individuals to fear and despise.

Hong Kong was a city filled with escapees from China, the British feeling it was very unsporting to refuse entry to anyone fleeing Communism. Milton and Michael of course were their own very singular category, being refugees from their father's repression, but once inside its borders, they would have no trouble blending into the teeming human anthill of activity that's Hong Kong. They would encounter many obstacles but being instantly recognizable among the hurrying, side-stepping crowd wasn't one of them, the twins just being two more souls dispersed in the twirl and whirl of tens of thousands of others in similar straits trying to find a life, keep a life, and maintaining that life as long as feasibly possible.

For the twins, it was no longer a fantasy; they had reached Hong Kong, the city's neon skyline towering above their now diminutive yet still mighty tramp. Milton leaned against the deck railing, watching all the action, worrying about how they would ever get past that vast assemblage of querulous custom officials standing on the pier below, subjecting new arrivals to intense questioning, thoroughly searching all incoming bags and personal belongings.

What Milton saw as insurmountable, the good captain knew just as part of the process, introducing his five wards as his own quintuplets, literally announcing to his new family to "Follow Daddy!" leading his children down the gang plank and past the now chuckling agents onto the firm concrete foundation that was the British Crown Colony, one sum in part of a larger empire and commonwealth reaching around a greater circumference.

Again, another victory achieved! Here they both were, walking in Hong Kong, yes, and alive, not murdered in a Saigon alley, drowned in the Mekong or some other similarly awful fate. They couldn't have been happier. And let's also not forget a few cheers for Tall Tong, that superior representative of the lower tier of the criminal classes. The twins literally owed him their lives, their relief going beyond any verbal expression. They had difficulty believing how well it had all worked out. Now that they had safely arrived, it was time to find a place to stay.

They had expected to find their cousin Jimmy from Saigon, now also a waiter at Tai Tung, awaiting them, but failed to find him at the assigned address. With that deflating news taking some of the shine off of their initial enthusiasm, they opted for an alternate plan that worked nearly as well. Having the address of an old Ky Con neighbor, the father of someone Milton had occasionally dated, they decided to try their luck.

The man was jubilant, thrilled to see his old neighbors, kindly welcoming them into his home. His hospitality lasted nearly a month, though quickly expiring after Wainam failed to respond back to his inquiring letters. Growing suspicious, and worried that they had entered Hong Kong illegally, he kicked the rascals out, but not before he found them a small, inexpensive sleeping room. All this activity occurred in January of 1964, the New Year finding Milton and Michael languishing in their tiny room, wondering what to do next, what new trouble could they possibly involve themselves in.

A welcome diversion soon appeared in the person of their congenial American buddy, Jim, who true to his word, came to Hong Kong on his first R&R, delivering the rest of the twins' money. Unfortunately, also remaining true to their less sensible sides, they proceeded to spend as much of it as they could during Jim's three-day-long sojourn, emulating the worst of their Saigon days. It appears they found it easier to compound earlier errors than discover any kind of positive lesson, this made all the more interesting given what they had just endured, now helplessly espousing a nonsensical philosophy of making what is fallacious correct by habitual repetition.

Despite their recent carousing, the twins understood that they were essentially marooned in Hong Kong, and without someone's direct intervention, fated to stay there indefinitely. Feeling that their salvation rested in the hands of their far luckier siblings, they began a telephone and letter campaign pleading their case, asking for help. They felt a new kind of desperation, the situation in Hong Kong beyond their combined experience, surpassing anything they knew, now faceless in a teeming human sea.

What they needed was a Hong Kong version of Tall Tong, an able surrogate or substitute, and luckily, one was on her way: someone as plump as he was thin, capable of sweetening the sour and correcting the seasonings, tossing the twins' burnt offerings into the nearest rubbish bin.

Soon after Jim's departure, Auntie Wong, the one true heroine of this story, made her debut, not only saving the day, but also preserving their immediate futures, because, in all probability, the twins would have remained permanently in Hong Kong without her charitable interventions. In reality, the heroic Auntie Wong wasn't their aunt at all, but their sister Victoria's mother-in-law, a Chinese-American permanently residing in Hong Kong summoned to the twins as their supreme rescuer.

Auntie Wong, her pampered Pekinese in tow, arrived at their room without warning, totally unannounced, surprising Milton and Michael out of a depressive stupor. Bearing the persona of a good shepherdess, she was fully prepared to guide her wandering lambs to more palatial stables, providing instantaneous comfort and serenity to two wayward souls in sore need of unction and just plain, unadorned affection.

Auntie Wong, originating from San Francisco, California, reputed to be married to a wealthy Hong Kong vintner and winery owner, was a woman now in her mid-fifties completely free of all economic pressures, her only maternal concerns the aforementioned Pekinese, a spoiled creature partial to dim sum. Whether her current husband was her first or tenth I have no information, along with not knowing how many children she had, though obviously having at least one son, name unknown. Though the twins stayed with their adoptive auntie for nearly five months, I have no clues concerning the whereabouts or description of her wine-imbued husband. Given that he has never been mentioned I suspect he might have been buried in the garden but living in a high-rise condominium I suppose she didn't have one.

This all added up to a woman with lots of time and very little to do, much in need of a hobby, which is what Milton and Michael became: a kind of self-designed philanthropic project, her new "nephews" in dire need of careful guidance and instruction. Many years in that crowded city had provided her with an intimate awareness of its manners and contradictions, having successfully negotiated herself countless times into and through the various bureaucratic byways and mazes necessary to get anything officially done. Permits, licenses, visas, documents of any kind were not just handed out. Instead, a kind of institutionalized formality existed, knowing what and how to say it tantamount, ritual all important if you wanted a particular piece of paper issued, style counting as much as substance. Why do anything if it couldn't be done politely and correctly?

Auntie Wong was the perfect choice to politely bulldoze anything through the entrenched bureaucratic mind. Being both Chinese and American gave her considerable leverage. Her American-accented English and tone allowed her to sidestep much ingrained resistance. Being rich, and befitting her social position, dressing like a dowager queen—her ample body wrapped in satin and bedecked with precious stones and jewels—loudly signaled to any and all petty officials to watch out, her highness Auntie Wong was now approaching, and though bowing wasn't mandatory, it was at least advisable. This attitude served the twins well, certainly needing someone like her in their lives: a combination mother and father figure, plus friend and benefactress all in one slightly obese package. Auntie Wong didn't mind. The twins were nearly as well behaved as her beloved Pekinese.

The safe haven Auntie Wong herded the twins to, though not

quite a lush, green pasture was something more appropriate for the dense, urban jungle that is Hong Kong, an amply furnished and spacious flat located on one of the upper floors of an imposing skyscraper. Hong Kong, similar to Manhattan, contains more vertical than horizontal space. In the short term, Milton and Michael had few worries, room and board at least now taken care of. It was the more immediate future that posed problems, details of which they were little aware. Thankfully, Victoria's letter described in detail the twins' history and plight, pleading for her mother-in-law's assistance. Auntie Wong understood the task ahead, quickly going forward looking for solutions. Time was something the twins were running out of, given their United States entry visas would expire on their twenty-first birthdays, a scant nine months away. Failing to meet that deadline would only mean further bureaucratic obstacles. No one needed that. Auntie Wong had to get to work.

Auntie Wong devised a plan. The twins would have to become mainland Chinese, posing as refugees escaping Communism's iron yoke. Since she had just met them, she probably didn't quite understand what she was undertaking: attempting to mold two such recalcitrant young men into something they held little capacity to become. In reality, or their distorted version of it, they didn't want to know anything, acting like the ennobled upper class they were brought up to be: people who did little individually for themselves, others, servants for instance doing it for them. Cooperation, for the twins, was a foreign word, not part of their learned vocabulary. Coercion they did understand, their father in that regards a good and able teacher.

Milton and Michael, despite their father's abuse, were incredibly spoiled human beings, and having been injured, angry at the world, disinclined toward personal responsibility. In their eyes, to be given things was a natural right accorded to them as obvious superior entities.

If their actions require further explanation, this attitude again tells why, apart from their desperation, they involved themselves in cheating Ding and his invisible compatriots. Simply, they deserved that money, it being their anointed right to have it. A fairly unsavory and selfish outlook, and unkind, clearly mirroring their wonderful father. These kinds of ingrained attitudes, now innate, did not make them the best candidates for arduous learning. All they wanted to do was get to Seattle and have fun, little else, America just one large continuous amusement park, where no one pays and everything is free, the fabled land of milk and honey and perpetual Social Security.

It was obvious that they couldn't tell the truth, telling any British colony official the real story would only result in a one-way ticket back to Saigon. However reluctantly, with Auntie Wong's Chinese maid as their primary instructor, they began their lessons on how to be mainland Chinese. Unfortunately, the maid-cum-cultural coach could only teach what she was most familiar with, that being of the more domestic and local sciences: how to best choose a duck, knowing the current price of salt, the name of the local ferry or which train takes you from Guangzhou (Canton) to Hong Kong. All of this being all well and good in its limited context, but certainly falling far short of what would be needed to fool a legion of stern questioners intent on tripping up all less-than-candid applicants, a category matching the twins' prevalent attitude and current position.

It was decided that they would pose as Guangzhou high school students, having come from a village somewhere in the countryside. It might have been helpful, a good start, to at least know the name of this mythical home village. You might now see that being tied to the maid's apron strings may not have been the most fortuitous bond. To achieve Auntie Wong's goal would have taken careful tutoring, not the haphazard dispensing of useless information to uninterested students. Milton later became a good cook, even owning a restaurant. Maybe the genesis began with the maid's teaching. It's doubtful he learned anything beyond how much cornstarch makes a proper sauce or when to add MSG, Auntie Wong's miscalculation turning into something much larger once classes were terminated, when Milton and Michael faced questioning by someone who actually knew the answers.

Interspersed between the twins' tutoring sessions were walks with their Auntie and the Pekinese, usually to lunch at her brother's sprawling Chinese dim sum restaurant. It seems an argument with the Internal Revenue Service over the taxation of his gambling ventures in San Francisco's Chinatown had resulted in a quick vacation somewhere down in Mexico. Eventually, after a few days peaceful reflection, he decided that relocating to Hong Kong was the best resolution to an honest disagreement. After the rousing success of his restaurant, he decided to make his transition permanent, Hong Kong being pleased to have his business investments. Milton says the dim sum was excellent.

After a month's more or less training, the diligent students of everything "Chinese" appeared, or maybe it just was Auntie Wong's wishful thinking, to be ready to face Hong Kong's dreaded immigration officials. The twins' official storyline was as follows.

Disgruntled with the educational opportunities offered in Guangzhou, the southern Chinese city also known as Canton, they fled to Hong Kong for the greater academic freedoms offered in a free society. Now that they were here, they wished to stay, resuming their studies as soon as possible.

Though Auntie Wong appears to have been far more responsible than her brother, she might have shared a predilection for myth and fable, or even better, for authoring it yourself. That the twins didn't even know the location or address of their supposed alma mater appeared to have neither deterred nor fazed anyone concerned. What did she think they were going to be asked, where to buy the finest cotton batting? Her approach seemed a trifle nonsensical—not that they would have noticed, the twins frozen in a very personalized suspended animation, quite fruitless to ask their opinion as they didn't have one, sleepwalking from one event to the next, fully believing that they were preordained to grace the streets of Seattle.

It was a fateful day in late April 1964, when the good Auntie Wong led her anxious charges down to the Territorial Immigration Building to formally apply for permanent residency status, the first in a number of steps needed toward the ultimate goal of leaving Hong Kong legally for the United States. By leaving South Vietnam in the manner recently described, the twins at best had delayed an inevitable process, replacing one massive bureaucracy for the other, but this one far more dangerous, being organized and efficient, thereby making it potentially lethal. Now they were up against it, facing the consequences of their own actions. Instead of walking back out with Auntie Wong, they might be arrested and taken away in handcuffs. As they were ushered into a small office, Milton was suddenly ill as the door closed, shutting them off from the very freedom they had come so far to embrace.

As if scripted, or at the very least, the repetition of a well-known scenario, a short, swarthy man, possibly Portuguese, silently entered the room, and minus any visible emotion stared at the twins, quietly appraising these new refugees, a knowledgeable cat teasing the dumbfounded mice, enjoying their discomfort, watching them squirm beneath his dark gaze. Like any cat, he was in no hurry.

Time stopped. The world stood still. The only sound to be heard in the room was the twins breathing, and of course, the customary ticking of the clock. Milton and Michael were doomed. It was all over and done with. They knew it.

The immigration official continued his silent, deadly unnerving estimation, pacing back and forth, each step minutely inching him forward, until finally stopping a foot away, towering over the now cowering twins. He was ready.

"Where," he demanded, speaking in fluent Cantonese, "where

are you two from? I want to know. Now!"

The twins responded the best they could, saying they were high school students from Guangzhou, having recently arrived to live with their aunt. They told him how they wanted to attend school in Hong Kong.

The inspector appeared skeptical, obviously unconvinced. "Everyday," he began, "everyday I interview hundreds of Chinese from every part of China. You don't look nor act like any of them. My guess is that you are from somewhere in Southeast Asia. Maybe you have come from Cambodia. Or is it Vietnam? Wherever you are from, it certainly isn't China. I doubt if you have actually been there. This will only work if you tell me the truth. I need to know where you came from."

Like human parrots, having been taught only one complete sentence, they kept repeating that they were from Guangzhou and no where else. They had no other response because they hadn't been given one. Disgusted, or perhaps only feigning distaste, the inspector said, "Okay, I'll make a deal with you. Answer three simple questions for me and you'll receive your residency papers. Do you lads understand?"

The twins nodded, answering that they understood.

"First," he asked, "how many young men like you are drafted each year into the Chinese Army?"

They replied that since they never left the dormitory, they didn't know any soldiers. They also said that they knew nothing about the Chinese army. On this point at least they were telling the truth.

"Okay, okay," he responded, "that was too difficult. Since you're both from Guangzhou, this one should be easy. I'm sure you've been there many times. Tell me, where is Jun Sung Park?"

They responded that they were sorry to disappoint him, but as they were confined to their dormitories, they had never visited the aforementioned park. They only had time for study.

He again just stared at them, obviously losing his patience, which was understandable. They were lying and he knew it. He also was beginning to frequently check his watch. By either design or happenstance, Auntie Wong had chosen a late hour as the office was just minutes from closing. This might have worked in the twins' favor.

Shaking his head, he said, "Okay, I'm sure you two arrived by ship. Answer this correctly and we will be through, and you'll be able to remain in Hong Kong. How many harbors does the port of Guangzhou have? Answer that and you're free to go."

The sorry truth was that neither of them knew where Guangzhou was actually located. Not only could they not locate it on a map, they didn't know whether it was landlocked or located on a river, the maid's lessons evidently failing to cover local geography. Milton was afraid that he was trying to trick them, catch them in a lie, as if he hadn't already done that. This time they said they had come directly from the countryside; that they didn't know much about the city itself.

That was glaringly apparent. Tiring of their evasions, he told them that they had better start being honest or he would have them arrested. He then left the room, leaving Milton and Michael to confer amongst themselves.

Angrily whispering, they argued back and forth, Milton insisting that they stay with their original story, finally agreeing on a new variation, having entered Hong Kong from the Portuguese territory of Macau. Logically, that didn't explain anything but at this juncture they were in complete despair, only expecting the worst.

Upon returning and hearing their new story, the inspector laughed, shaking his head, suddenly in a good mood. Looking up at the wall clock and noting the time, told the twins it was time to go home. Briskly returning to the desk where the applications in question lay waiting, said in English to the utterly shocked twins, "Congratulations," as he repeatedly stamped their forms, "you two are now official subjects of the Queen. Now do try to behave yourselves."

After telling them they would have to come back in the morning to receive their security clearances, he added that he hoped they wouldn't get lost if they ever attempted a return to their hometown. That was it, the twins now free to officially do whatever they wanted, a somewhat abrupt end to the most important interview of their young lives. They were stunned, not understanding what had just happened, achieving a victory that moments before had seemed beyond all hope. They were now barely able to get out of their chairs.

As with much of this story, why the inspector validated their claim will never truly be known, but I think it is easy to guess why. When he left the room, Auntie Wong intervened, giving him a donation he couldn't refuse. I can't think of another plausible explanation. What other possible motivation could exist except a monetary one? Perhaps some extreme empathy, but as the inspector said, he had seen refugees originating from all parts of China who must have been truly threadbare and indigent. Milton and Michael didn't quite match that description. Cheeky and disdainful maybe, but bereft of human comforts, no, too much recent dim sum a plump confirmation of their actual real-life condition.

Anyway, regardless of reason and explanation, the twins, with little time for celebration, were now facing part two, with no time for additional preparation. Not that it would have helped them. Theoretically, receiving their security clearances should have been routine, just more governmental posturing and paper shuffling, but given the afternoon's botched performance, nothing was guaranteed.

In their two-hundred-plus years of managing an Empire, the British had turned bureaucratic fussiness into a vexing science, an intrusive, institutionalized scrutiny matching the nose of your best English bloodhound. This worried Auntie Wong, making her determined to somehow remain throughout the next morning's proceedings. Nothing, she realized, when it came to these two, was preordained, finally seeing how vulnerable the twins were, nearly requiring as much protection as her beloved Pekinese— who at least had sharp teeth and an irritating bark.

Approximately fifteen hours later, Milton and Michael entered the Hong Kong police headquarters riding a crest of relative optimism, certainly minus the consternation felt the previous afternoon. After yesterday's near catastrophe, this day's interview seemed anticlimactic, almost not worth attending. Surviving a visit to the lion's lair colored everything a paler shade, muting their apprehension. If anything, they were actually somewhat confident, their optimism registering a slight pulse.

Milton and Michael, along with Auntie Wong, now acting as their official interpreter, were ushered into a large office filled with at least twenty hard wooden chairs, possibly the setting for expanded tribunals, but thankfully that day nearly empty except for the two very sullen Chinese police officers awaiting their entry. They appeared to be decidedly grumpy, as if they had missed their morning coffee and it was all the twins' fault.

Similar to the previous day's interview, this also had a contrived quality, something spontaneously scripted for the occasion. One actor sat irritably slumped behind an imposing document laden desk. The other remained standing, pacing at an angle opposite the politely waiting trio: a staccato dance building in improvised fury.

The dancer gave the twins' papers a dismissive glance, tossing them back upon the desk.

"I want you to know," he scolded in Chinese, "that we know you are lying. Wherever you've come from, it's not from China. Your skin is too dark. Your hair is too curly. And where did you get those clothes? You two are obviously lying. I am going to ship the both of you back to Macau, and you can rot there!"

Milton and Michael just sat there in wordless terror, battered by the officer's verbal abuse. Auntie Wong remained expressionless, not uttering a sound, apparently awaiting her cue, her moment to perform. She didn't have long to wait.

The officer's roaring crescendo, or was it bad acting, brought his superior, a captain, into the room, quietly inquiring just what was going on?

This momentary lull allowed the ever-courageous Auntie Wong to rise, making her full, ample entry into the ongoing melodrama. Turning and facing the captain directly, ignoring the officers as commonplace chaff, she broke into a bereaved grandiloquence. "Sir," she began, in perfectly enunciated English, her voice both compelling and sweet, "the nature of this interview has heretofore been grossly and singularly unfair. I'm quite surprised you allow your officers to conduct themselves in such a manner. My nephews risked their lives escaping from that awful China, now only to be treated this disrespectfully. It's utterly disgraceful. I believe I will be forced to file a formal complaint. Instead of this horrible grilling, my nephews should be issued medals!"

With that one bravura performance literally taking the breath out of the room, there was truly nothing left to be said nor done, the decision already understood. The captain, arching his eyebrows, glanced toward his lieutenants, nodded and left the room without speaking another word. The officers obediently filled out the necessary forms, stamping and stiffly handing them over to the twins. Dumbfounded, they could barely mutter thank you. And with that, Auntie Wong got them quickly out of there before anything else happened, greatly relieved, ready for a pot of tea and her brother's dim sum!

Now with the fear of deportation removed, Auntie Wong could now concentrate on that important final step, getting the twins onto American soil. In preparation for this moment, their mother had transferred their American visas to Hong Kong. All they had to do now was to wait for all the documents from the Immigration offices to arrive, and then they could leave, Olga paying for their flight to Seattle. Unfortunately, Auntie Wong grew impatient; overly concerned that everything wouldn't be in order before the twins' birthday in October.

Her new bright idea, though ultimately successful, nearly scuttled the entire process by not understanding that the information on their visas directly contradicted much that had been told to the Hong Kong authorities. They were going to have problems anyway with the obvious contradictions. By adding yet another bureaucracy into the mix, she innocently complicated the twins' process.

Her new thought was to make Milton and Michael citizens of Taiwan, thinking this would quicken their departure, though I don't understand why. The twins of course didn't care, always agreeing with their good Auntie Wong. If she wanted them to fill out some more official forms and send them off to the Taiwanese consulate in Macau, they were in agreement with that. Didn't Auntie Wong know best?

The entire month of May passed with nary a word from Macau. Was something wrong? Had Auntie Wong somehow miscalculated? In early June the answer to her anxieties came with a knock upon the door. Standing there was a courteous gentleman, a representative of the Nationalist government, and could he come in as he had a few questions. What the consulate staff found puzzling was the discrepancies in the various sets of documents. One listed their birthplace as China, another as South Vietnam. There were obvious contradictions. What the official needed to know now was the truth.

Auntie Wong immediately understood her error, realizing it was time to end the ongoing deceits and be completely honest, telling the not unsympathetic official how all of this business had been quite unnecessary, all caused by the callousness of an uncaring father. He listened intently, asking the twins a few pertinent questions, promising he would do what he could, but please understand that he could not offer any guarantees.

Whatever was going to happen would, unalterable circumstances were now in play and proceeding to unknown conclusions. Again without options, as usual, the twins would have to wait.

In the end, it appears empathy won out, as about two weeks later the twins' new passports arrived. Almost not believing it, they were now free to go, their ordeal over, soon to be in their symbolic city of Oz, Seattle, Washington, USA. Auntie Wong, while not quite a wizard, certainly deserved the title of minor miracle-maker, having lifted the twins up and over and past all obstacles to where they needed to be. She had done something extremely rare, giving them the real opportunity to create something genuinely positive and new in their lives. With her blessings, they were now free to roam the big, wide world.

On August 8, 1964, nearly nine months after leaving that Saigon street corner, they reached the United States, landing at Seattle-Tacoma International Airport. A cool, almost cold breeze told Milton that he had indeed arrived at someplace foreign to his experience, far beyond his immediate comprehension. He was now going to be an American. For the very first time, he got what he wanted. What it all meant, he didn't know. Now two months short of his 21st birthday, it was time, if there ever was one, to embrace the future that he was now literally standing on.

Everything now, from his next step, would be new to him, the sidewalks, the streets, the thousands of new faces. Every day would contain an adventure. Like every immigrant whom had arrived before him, he was an explorer investigating a new world, only holding rough concepts of what awaited. Thankfully he had his brothers and sisters to temper his transition. Finally, for the very first time, minus any barriers, Milton would be with his family. This was a great moment. This was an important time, the beginning of hours growing into days, months and years blossoming into the life partially recorded in the story you are now reading.

The Ravenna neighborhood house, Milton's first home in Seattle.

Moon Temple Restaurant, Seattle's Wallingford neighborhood.

Yen Wor Garden Restaurant, formally The Tea House, in Seattle's Greenwood neighborhood. Milton's introduction to waiting tables.

Six

Finally Seattle: Working to 3 AM & Learning about this Unusual Place called America

Milton's earliest memories of Seattle and the Pacific Northwest are of unending rain and never being warm; and since he's making reference to the month of August, generally the hottest month of the year, this appropriately describes his initial introduction to a very new world. Everything indeed was different, America seeming so much larger and louder, a culture devoid of the reserved restraint he knew and in which he felt comfortable. Security, as he understood it, disappeared, the very foundation shifting beneath him, upsetting an already fragile equilibrium.

During his first few months in the United States, he had no idea where he was. Seattle, yes, he was in a city called Seattle, and that was about the extent of his understanding. His visions of a Perfect America had been promulgated by Technicolor movies, popular music and glossy magazines filled with beautiful faces. No one he saw looked remotely like Marilyn Monroe and Rock Hudson. Where were they hiding? And what about the white pillared mansions and long black Cadillacs driven by millionaires? He is still waiting to enter that mansion and shake hands with that ever-elusive millionaire.

Back in Saigon, Milton had imagined America as one giant

slot machine, a few quarters translating into an avalanche of coins. He was shocked, and perhaps still is, that the America he found was in reality the unfortunate opposite of what he had imagined and dreamt. Milton wanted the United States to be a Saturday matinee on a sunny afternoon. Instead he discovered a film slightly out of focus, minus of course the buttered popcorn.

The biggest disappointment might have been the racial discrimination he found living and breathing all around him, suddenly the color of his skin making him less human in the eyes of many. Of all his expectations, this was one he had never considered, never thinking why Hollywood would use a Caucasian (white) actor to portray a Chinese detective named Charlie Chan, suddenly remembering that all those Army officers he met were white, not a black man or someone of another color among them. Milton had never heard about the internment of the Japanese-Americans, or the maltreatment of the nineteenth-century Chinese laborers who had worked on the railroads. No one told him about the 1882 Chinese Exclusion Act or the 1924 Johnson-Reed Act that set ethnic quotas based on your national origin. It was all news to him and the news was bad, certainly not the America he thought he knew from the movie newsreels sitting in a darkened theater.

Now that he saw the truth in the daylight of a typically grey Seattle day, he didn't have a clear response. Thank goodness he had his family and Seattle's greater Chinese community to buffer him from the prevailing racial reality. Milton would never truly assimilate into the general American culture until he was drafted and entered that instant melting pot known as the United States Army, where racial equality in 1967 was more or less an everyday fact of life.

In his first days and months, Milton found America be a far more complex undertaking than just eating hamburgers, adding catsup and mustard and taking a big bite, the American menu quite extensive, pages and pages of offerings requiring a few minutes reading before motioning to the waitress and placing your order. Though most importantly, regardless of location, Milton was free (at least physically, the psychological being another issue) of his father's yoke, allowing him to make his own decisions minus any opinion his father might have had. Milton's gains and errors would truly be on his own time. He was now the responsible adult. He was now the autonomous human being making his own decisions; be them good or bad or catastrophic.

Milton and Michael's first residence in Seattle couldn't have been more welcoming and friendly. His sister Victoria, financially assisted by their mother, had created what could be described as a kind of Wan Family resettlement camp in Seattle's Ravenna neighborhood, a big yellow house large enough for all her wandering siblings. The younger brothers Samuel and Rodney were already there, along with their sister Marie and her entire family, everyone having their own rooms. For Milton, it was a dream come true: a room he didn't have to share.

Much of the monetary upkeep for this teeming community was provided by their mother's successful business ventures back in Saigon, Olga (despite her husband) ever mindful of her children's needs. Eventually, in 1975, with the imminent defeat of the South Vietnamese government near as enemy forces quickly progressed toward Saigon, Olga finally packed up, happily rejoining her family at the yellow house.

Eventually, Wainam too also found his way to America but taking a slightly more circuitous routing, first living again in France for eighteen months before joining his children in Seattle, living out his last days in the same yellow house Milton and Michael had first called home. I suppose there is a kind of irony contained in Wainam's final decisions. It just seems that he didn't consider that his actions were open to examination, any decision or past behavior was fine because he was never to be questioned or criticized. That this book is largely a response to that attitude makes it clear how well his persona ultimately served him, having bequeathed a less than positive legacy. Like so many self-appointed rulers, his imagined authority and territory had vanished beneath him, disappearing like an early morning mist on a warming day. Wainam, now removed from his foundation, was destined to live out his days in a tarnished and confused exile, memories stored away upon that infamous and forgotten dusty shelf. Where he is buried has never been mentioned. I can only imagine his final epitaph eroding away upon a weathered stone.

A new acceleration had entered Milton's life, now in quick transition from idle boy to responsible adult. Within a week, he found himself employed as a waiter at the Tea House Chinese restaurant, at the time the lone Chinese food establishment in Seattle's Greenwood neighborhood, a rough-hewn, blue-collar working-class district featuring small clapboard houses, occasionally surrounded by peeling (and sagging) wooden fences. The Tea House would prove to be a somewhat startling introduction to all things American. There was certainly nothing genteel about the Greenwood, having a blunt, in-your-face quality that's hard to appreciate unless you're drunk, which is what many of the first Americans he met in the United States were, drunk and obnoxious, by no stretch of the imagination in control of themselves, as ready for a round of fisticuffs as anything else.

To say the least, this was a new breed of American; very unlike those Milton had known in Saigon, their verbose profanity repelling him. They didn't seem to care about anything except drinking beer and groping each other. It was extremely disturbing, like going to a theater on a rainy day expecting a romance and instead finding yourself immersed in a horror film. This was not the America of his daydreams. It was appalling. And these denizens of course were his customers, people he had to be nice to. It was beyond his comprehension that Americans could act like this. It was time for a dramatic reassessment that continues today.

Sometimes while sitting at the Tai Tung counter, I observe Milton's interactions with some of our cultures' more belligerent citizens. I can sense the ongoing internal struggle he is having. "Why do I have to keep dealing with these people!" is Milton's clear reaction. Yes, and after they insult him to his very fiber, they don't leave a tip either! Oh well, what can you do, sometimes life is unkind regardless of all best efforts put forward.

All of this was a bit too sudden for him, this instantaneous metamorphosis into a waiter. Poor Milton, now treated like a box of that favorite All-American dessert, Jell-O pudding—adding water and mixing, then unceremoniously plopped directly into the refrigerator. But in reality he had instead been inserted into a fiery furnace—like Sam McGee toasting his feet in the boiler on the marge of Lake Labarge---never fated to fully cool down.

Michael too was meeting the same fate, his assignment being the Moon Temple, a restaurant located in the much nicer Wallingford neighborhood, a mile due west of the University of Washington. His clientele was slightly more intellectual, sipping their cocktails instead of guzzling themselves into modified oblivion.

In general, it is accurate to say that Michael's transition was far more tranquil, as I have mentioned, being less emotional than his temperamental twin, enabling him to better adjust to difficult situations. For Milton, everything was a personal insult, an attack upon his very identity. Oppositely, Michael somehow was able to ignore much of the nonsense sent in his direction. Though physically similar, that's where it ended, both having developed very distinct personalities. If Milton was all exterior, coming apart at the seams, Michael was the interior opposite, his emotions submersed, contained within a compliant façade, his code of conduct being not to stir the waters, preferring a smooth glide across a becalmed lake. No Loch Ness monsters for Michael, avoiding Scotland altogether. Let Milton deal with all those nasty creatures up in the Greenwood, that not being Michael's cup of baked Oolong Chinese tea.

This is also when their uneasy allegiance, forged over so many unhappy childhood years ended, sadly breaking down to a rivalry that on various levels still exists today. Maybe it was the strain of keeping up a united front against their father. Like herding animals, one found a kind of safety in numbers. It was better than being completely alone. Of course there was the natural dimension of needing to form individual identity but that is only part of the explanation.

For whatever assorted and various reasons, a stylistic schism opened a breach that has only widened over the ensuing years, each on the opposite side of a gaping canyon. Again, just another reminder of the sorry legacy bequeathed by an unthinking father whose only concern was his immediate self. If the Wans were a more verbally expressive family, possibly they would have eventually achieved some form of reconciliation, but that isn't their way, not how they do things.

And at this late date, nearly forty-five years later, as far as I know, not one family member has asked Milton about his tremendous ordeal or the amazing journey that you have just read in the previous chapter. This story is as much news to them as it has been for you, a complete stranger who just happens to be reading this book.

Whatever one may wish to call this lack, or style of communication, it certainly can not be called a particularly positive trait. Without this book, his family probably would have gone to the grave never knowing the true extent of Milton and Michael's story. And I am guessing that they wished that I had never brought the topic up. My defense is that Milton's story deserves to be heard, whether anyone wants to hear or know it. Silence on serious matters will always be a kind of injustice. Some matters just have to be discussed. There is no alternative.

Clearly, Seattle's Chinese business community embraced the cultural concept of a greater family, making every attempt to assist new arrivals like the twins. Waiting tables may not be the most pleasant occupation but at least it was honest, sustaining work, one rung on the ladder toward an upper mobility. From this genesis a stable personal and cultural foundation was built.

Later on, after the Army, Milton began managing restaurants and eventually owning one himself. That was the communities' plan, instilling a cultural pride and cohesion, making all those important steps forward possible. Another reason this happened was simply history, the Chinese remembering the injustice and abuse directed at them. They knew that the only people they could trust to help the newly arrived immigrants were themselves, not depending on anyone else to care.

Seattle's Chinese and the Asian community in general have expanded considerably since Milton's arrival. The Vietnamese, most having arrived after the conclusion of the Vietnam War, have especially strived, their community spreading east of the Chinatown/International District proper to what is now called "Little Saigon."

With that area now saturated, the Vietnamese have expanded southeast into the various neighborhoods of greater Rainier Valley, once an Italian truck-farming area affectionately known as "Garlic Gulch." You won't have any problems finding a Vietnamese restaurant there or elsewhere in Seattle. Thai restaurants are everywhere too, especially popular in the University district. If you are searching for Filipino cuisine, take a right off of South Jackson onto 12th Avenue South and head up to Beacon Hill, another area of new Asian immigrant expansion.

Currently, their East African counterparts, that newest wave of immigrants coming to Seattle, originating primarily from Ethiopia, Eritrea and Somalia, are undergoing a similar assimilation. Weekly it appears a new Ethiopian restaurant is popping up on another corner in the neighborhoods just east, north and south of the greater International District, ready to feed the legions of young men trying their luck behind the wheel of a taxi. Like the twins before them, except 45 years later, they too are attempting to decipher this riddle called America, home to both unlimited opportunities and frustrations, simultaneously shouting with joy while tearing out their hair.

If the complex task of becoming acclimated to a nearly alien culture wasn't enough of a challenge, within a mere two weeks of their arrival the twins both received some unwelcome greetings from their Uncle Sam, requesting the pleasure of their company at a Selective Service pre-induction center. They were shocked, and that is a huge understatement, not understanding how this could happen, this sudden intrusion into their new lives. Hadn't they just arrived a few minutes prior to this rude invitation?

Quickly it seemed, their American honeymoon was over, learning that living in the United States held many surprises, some of which, especially this one, might be termed unpleasant. There they were, back in South Vietnam, worried about being drafted, and now, after their long journey, about to enter the US Army. They couldn't believe it, their American dream at least for the moment now a modified nightmare.

Even though the US military has justly earned the reputation of taking any warm body remaining vertical while simultaneously registering a slight pulse, they did have some small expectation that their soldiers could comprehend their sergeant's all-important commands. Maybe their father did them a favor after all by yanking them out of Father Louie's language school, as both Milton and Michael failed the Selective Services' very rudimentary language competency tests, thus delaying their transformation into able-bodied soldiers. They were told they would just have to come back when they spoke English nearly as well as the average American.

On top of that good news, Milton received something that should have been even better, a permanent medical deferment. The good government doctors, in their medical wisdom, had decided that he had diabetes. It was news to him. Milton thinks it was the half-dozen donuts he ate just prior to the pre-induction physical, somehow disrupting his blood sugar levels. Since he was confident he was healthy it should have been the greatest news, a gift from the heavens. Most young men in 1964 would have shouted for joy but not Milton.

Instead of elation, his overwhelming reaction was disappointment. How could that be, seemingly counterintuitive to all his hopes and ambitions? What had been revealed was a not so secret desire now shattered, the somewhat incomprehensible dream of one day being an American soldier. As irrational as that might sound, that is what he wanted to be, somehow representing a kind of pinnacle, the best he could possibly do and be, something not dissimilar to Stendhal's character from *The Red & The Black*, young Julien Sorel as he watched the Sixth Dragoons return from an Italian campaign, imagining himself among Bonaparte's proud ranks.

The psychology behind this wish was convoluted, not making much sense until closely examined. At this juncture, Milton really wasn't sure who he was. Was he Chinese, or then again, Vietnamese—but wasn't he really an American after all was said and done? He truly didn't know the answer himself, isolated on an island not quite of his own making, minus country or flag. And the truth was that he felt defeated, that he never would do anything well. Somehow, becoming an American soldier held a very special personal vindication, repairing his father's disappointment, atoning for a sin never committed. Overt emotion will never seem wholly logical. But this was not going to impede Milton, a blind determination compelling him forward.

Milton, for all the good reasons why he shouldn't, still felt that he was the guilty party, everything remaining his fault. Like it was for Mister Humpty-Dumpty who fell off a wall, the United States Army, minus all the horses and king's men, would be the glue that would put him back together again. It was an interesting concept originating from an identity crisis run amok, a frenzied soul galloping in circles. It might be said that at this juncture Milton was somewhat confused, simultaneously hitting himself while shaking his own hand, a difficult and contradictory maneuver to achieve even once, let alone maintain day after day.

It then became Milton's new paramount mission in life to have this erroneous diagnosis corrected, to again become draft eligible. It was all pretty simple. Go to a private physician but this time avoiding the donuts. This he did and soon thereafter receiving the good news that he was once again a prime target for the United States Army. All he had to do now was improve his English elocution and wait for his number to come up. Milton couldn't have been happier. Eventually he would become, on some bright future day, an American soldier prepared to salute a newly minted self, having shed his previous identity and skin.

It was a unique perspective, one I assume not shared by many during those harrowing times. Almost no one wanted to be drafted, Milton falling into a category that I'm sure Selective Service had no status for, Milton's attitude being singularly unusual—a willing candidate for the meat grinder, for the awaiting body bag. Or given the young man he was, unaware of the potentially fatal consequences awaiting him. But this is what happens when someone simplifies the complicated. You end up missing the entire story while simultaneously composing it. You have to be your own editor. For Milton something had definitely been lost in the translation from child to adult.

Anyone experienced in dealing with that sometimes confounding governmental machinery called the Selective Service System, like me for instance, quickly came to understand there was often little definable sense in their average decision making. Who knew what they were going to do? Personally, I know I didn't. Even when I told them that I would rather go to prison by refusing induction, they said that I would make a fine officer. Of course this kind of response was not impressive, only further heightening my youthful skepticism. My father's long tenure in the United States Navy and Navy Reserve told me that governmental institutions were not to be trusted. Twenty years later he was still a radar-man third-class. He didn't care but I found it insulting, clearly undervaluing a lifetime commitment. This was the military as I knew it, the institution Milton saw as his great redemption.

As for the twins, they unexpectedly received a three-year-long reprieve. Maybe Selective Service thought it would take a long time for them to grasp essential grammatical principles, or were they simply lost somewhere in the bureaucratic shuffle? Who knows because you can be sure that Selective Service didn't care one way or the other. The twins were only numbers to be counted, nothing else. But for whatever reason it couldn't have worked out better, allowing the both of them invaluable time to adjust to a very strange land. Seattle and the United States was now their home. No question about that. It was time to take a look around and see just what they had committed themselves to.

For Milton, waiting tables at the Tea House was an unpleasant revelation, a brisk introduction into a world he had only frequented as a customer though now thrust into an unimaginable, chaotic drudgery six days a week. Beginning in the late afternoon until finally collapsing sometime past 3 AM, he faced an endless assembly line of chicken chow mein, egg foo yung and sweet and sour spare ribs delivered to a decidedly uncivil crew. This was work, hard work in its clearest definition.

This period, though he didn't know it, was the beginning of a lifetime of working in restaurants, cooking, managing, and eventually owning a place in Burien, Washington. The Tea House for him was a kind of introductory crash-course: Chinese Restaurant 101, in everything that cooking and serving could be. There was no choice but to learn quickly on the job, doing it as well as could be done, with obviously no time for formal instruction expect possibly a few quick shouts yelled in your general direction. You either were a waiter or not, there existed no in betweens—the infamous "sink or swim" school of vocational training. Milton, to his surprise, discovered that he was a waiter, something instinctive, though how or why he couldn't tell you. Did he like it? He didn't know that answer either, too busy to think about it.

Another confounding dimension to his new life in America, to this crazy restaurant business, was the endless stream of inebriated customers, those bedraggled, profane men and woman flooding into the Tea House between midnight and three in the morning, the fabled and dreaded bar rush, stumbling and falling down, vomiting in the restrooms, even falling asleep "face first" in their beef chop suey. This was typical of the Greenwood neighborhood, to find America's "mighty workforce" passed out, unconscious upon the barroom floor, a tradition maintained into the new century, the year 2009 not dissimilar to 1964.

Milton truly couldn't believe it, every Friday and Saturday night a repetition of the same old story, the same repeat customers knocking their plates off the counter and not even saying sorry. And you were supposed to keep smiling? It wasn't possible but he smiled anyway.

Were these the same Americans he had once so admired, he asked himself? He had to laugh, these awful people bearing scant resemblance to the polite, sartorially sharp American and French businessmen visiting Ky Con Street. Milton had no idea where these particular Americans came from, or how they had been created, an alien breed, a feral aberration. It was an America he had never imagined and here it was, walking into the Tea House talking to him. He wanted to run away but there was no place to go. He was there and would have to make the best of it. What could he really say? He had got what he wanted and that's the end to that story; be it good or bad, he was in Seattle. Now if only it would stop raining and the cold wind blowing!

Milton's life got even busier; taking on a schedule only a young body could manage, adding English language courses to his morning routine after his now usual 4 to 5 hours sleep. It helped immensely living with his brothers and sister, a congenial beehive, all busy making a new life for themselves. This is what Milton had wanted his entire childhood, to belong to the coming and goings of a happy household. It made everything easier, even commuting five miles south to his classes at a vocational school located at 22nd South and South Jackson in Seattle's Central District.

Milton soon joined that very American rite of passage: learning to drive an automobile, specifically, his brother Edmond's 1959 Chevrolet Impala bravely chaperoned by same said brother. After a mere one month's instruction, Milton took his first motor vehicle driving test out of the then Green Lake Department of Licensing office, located in a part of the city infamous for its maze of confusing, not to say confounding variety of four-way and five-way stops. After three adventurous attempts, Milton finally received his first driving license. Soon thereafter, a family friend sold him a huge 1958 Desoto, a chrome-plated monster of a car weighing nearly four thousand pounds, for $300 total, $100 down, and payments of $20 a month, interest not required.

It was in his Desoto that Milton learned the streets and neighborhoods of Seattle, sometimes taking a date to that most American of bygone venues, the drive-in theater, reacquainting him with the mythological America found solely on the silver screen. Afterwards, he would always stop at one of the Burgermasters, a local chain of drive-in restaurants, ordering his cheeseburger and French fries from attractive, adolescent carhops.

On occasions like these, it was definitely amusing getting to know his new home America, for the first time describing himself as happy. The Desoto was his personal "magic carpet," this giant chariot taking the diminutive five-foot-three, one-hundred-ten-pound Milton on many small adventures in and around the greater metropolitan area.

This period held a dual purpose. Not only was it an

obvious cultural transition but also an emotional awakening, a transformation from the child to the adult. These three years were a delayed adolescence, Milton a teenager about four years late, when mental and physical maturation collides headlong into pubescent awkwardness. Sometime during this transition he formed a reasonable adult identity, providing some ability to view himself not solely as a wounded child but better, as a functional adult. Milton's actual teenage years, his true chronological adolescence could perhaps be interpreted as little more than a shadow play, his best efforts silhouetted against a blank wall.

When not working and studying, Milton spent much of his idle time (and money) in the then-flourishing illegal gambling halls in the aforementioned International District/Chinatown, a traditional Asian shopping and dining area, a little bit of home for the local Chinese and Japanese immigrants. The Chinese fraternal or friendship associations provided both entertainment and refuge, a much-needed respite from an alien world. It was something Milton needed after his too many hours at the restaurant, arriving after bar-break and gambling until closing time, seven in the morning. Milton fondly remembers a tiny café offering an early sanctuary to him and the other nocturnal gamblers, serving spare ribs and Spanish-style squid, amongst other tempting dishes.

After about two years, Milton abruptly left the Tea House, joining Michael at the Moon Temple. After an ill-advised clash with a young female cashier, something about who had control over the cash register, he slapped her. This would make the first and last time Milton would strike someone. It wasn't something he wanted to repeat.

When the Tea House owner, who had become Milton's mentor and second father, failed to back his side of the argument, Milton left in a huff, thoroughly insulted. He felt disrespected and unappreciated, Wainam's legacy lurking beneath the surface, erupting like an unwelcome blemish, marring his recent tranquility.

That Milton could throw away such a potentially important sponsor said much concerning his internal life, tossed upon his own stormy sea. The owner had welcomed Milton into his own house, treating him like a family member. Maybe it was just too confusing to be treated respectfully by a paternal figure. Regardless, Milton never repaired that rupture, assigning it to the past. If there were any positives to this, it was leaving the Tea House's usual festive clientele behind, easier serving the hungry university students contemplating Sigmund Freud and Planck's Quantum Theory.

It was also around this same time that Milton left the cozy and protective confines of his sister's house and moved into his own apartment on Seattle's Capitol Hill. This gladly ended one was of his commutes, his home nearly adjacent to his new language school, Edison Technical, which a few years later became Seattle Central Community College. Milton's new roommates were two Chinese brothers from the Philippines, both fellow Edison classmates. His apartment, located just one block west off Broadway East, directly behind the famous Dick's Hamburgers, put him smack in the middle of Seattle's most urbane and diversified neighborhood, rubbing elbows with almost every kind of imaginable human being. This was not Ky Con Street, his eyes widening as he walked down that most eclectic of Seattle avenues, Broadway.

Milton's routine remained pretty much the same, working and going to school. Through his time at Edison he added a larger range of friends and acquaintances, in general growing more confident, adjusting to his new environment. His biggest struggle was with himself, fighting an ongoing internal battle. I don't believe visiting a psychotherapist was ever considered, a latent depression at times troubling but never completely debilitating. Anyway, as it turned out, the solution to all mental aberrations was just around the corner. Selective Service, that old friend, was about to tap him on the shoulder, curious to know if you, Mister Wan, could swear in English as efficiently as any other recruit?

In late January 1967, Milton received another draft notice, this time it all proved conclusive, now meeting all the requirements necessary to be conscripted into the United States armed forces. His wish had been granted. Milton was going be an American soldier. With casualties mounting, they needed everyone they could get. Milton and Michael, who had also received his notice, were now both deemed as qualified as any other average "American boy" next door. Uncle Sam really wasn't that fussy. There were boots to be filled and guns to be fired. America was at war.

Typical of the young Milton, he went down to the government induction center on the morning of May 14, 1967, thinking it was just some kind of informational meeting, not realizing he was about to be inducted into the United States Army. It was like going to the slaughterhouse not understanding you were about to be filleted. Instead of having breakfast, Milton found himself swearing an oath of allegiance to defend his new country, then quickly herded onto a bus taking him and his fellow conscripts 40 miles south to Fort Lewis, the biggest Army boot camp on the West Coast. Milton, without a doubt, and in some version of shock, was in the Army now, whizzing down Interstate 5 at 70 mph to a kind of military amusement park containing the usual entertainments and house of horrors.

Similar to Tall Tong's mysterious car ride nearly four years past, Milton had no idea what he had gotten himself into. As usual, he really hadn't given it much consideration, just giving himself up to fate. The only thing he did know for sure is that he wanted to be shipped off back to South Vietnam. No, not to battle the Communists but for reasons more personal, more private, reasons then still obscure to Milton, like the suicidal lemming, succumbing to an instinctual urge, initially faint but growing ever louder, edging ever closer to a looming abyss.

Posing with that "alien substance" snow at a wintry Fort Lewis.

Milton at Fort Lewis with his sister Victoria and family

Milton & soldier friend at Fort Lewis. Note position of Milton's rifle.

Milton at Victoria's house celebrating his boot camp graduation

Milton in his hotrod Oldsmobile 442.

Seven
Hello Shithead!
& Saluting Your
Local Laundry Matron

I have a pertinent question seeking an answer. Does anybody know, truly know why the American military (and certainly all the others in whatever foreign country) considers the brutalization of raw, young men reasonable, a positive originating from a negative? I know the various rationalizations but I am unconvinced that they serve as real answers.

When thought about, it's an interesting concept, treating people like absolute crap when your overall purpose is to instill a strident loyalty immune to any call other than blind duty to home and hearth. I think it must be a military translation of "spare the rod, spoil the child" applied to the everyday citizen-soldier, not wanting anyone to feel coddled.

Why, what kind of soldier would a pampered recruit make? Yes, one would hate to think what kindness instead might achieve, the open hand as an alternative to the clenched fist, to the shouted insult. But obviously, being drafted to be a potential killer of your fellow man is not about choice or free will or even common sense. It can only be about forcing someone to do something they wouldn't normally do, a kind of legal governmental kidnapping, saying to a young man that simply by being born you are now an indentured servant, minus any and

all options. Interestingly, Milton would find that the Army did
have an alternative when finding that socking him in the nose
wasn't the best or correct and effective incentive.

If Milton had suddenly changed his mind, deciding this wasn't
a very good idea after all, and had refused induction, he would
have faced five years of federal imprisonment, a loss of many
basic rights, and since he was still a green card holder, immediate
deportation back to South Vietnam. There was nothing benign
about the Selective Service System and the US Army back in
1967. There was government policy to enforce, a war to fight,
and woe to anyone questioning that authority. And this was the
system Milton now found himself immersed in, a raging river
rushing downstream to a turbulent sea, unconcerned what he
and the other recruits on that bus felt, all soon to be brave
soldiers clad in green, so big and handsome and ever so mean!

Other than wearing green fatigues, Milton would never truly
be identified with that rhyming, fighting machine. Oddly, he
never realized that he was just another expendable, easily replaced
part, never fully comprehending that his personal vision of the
military was mythical, an outlook created by deprivation, a thirsty
man washed upon a desert isle dreaming of a cool drink of water.
Sure, the water is wet, yet still not quite bubbly champagne. If the
entire experience had resulted in him returning in a body bag,
it would have meant nothing to the Army's overall functioning.
Milton would be dead, that's all, if one can be complacent about
an individual death, the Army continuing to live, and of course
kill. Milton would remain dead, never receiving any meaningful
appreciation of his ultimate sacrifice: no Milton Wan national
holidays, no special mention in the textbooks, his remembrance
less than the dust beneath your shoes.

By uttering a simple pledge of loyalty, Milton had become
a pawn, a sanctioned murderer, a warrior-cum-assassin for
American Democracy and for all democratic purposes in general.
He was definitely in the Army now, protecting me and you and

that patriotic pooch romping through golden wheat fields, Lassie in Kansas too!

Sitting on that bus, Milton imagined himself a nameless cow, remembering the unfortunate cattle on his Hong Kong voyage, sharing like them an unknown fate, suddenly feeling extremely alone on the hard, unyielding seat. Looking around, all he saw were blank faces, worried youths scared out of their wits. This is what he had asked for? Slowly he was beginning to understand how unrealistic his daydreams had been, awakening to an unimagined reality scary in its potential consequences.

Upon arrival at Fort Lewis, Milton quickly saw that the US Army ran on the strictest of timetables as they were all hurried off the buses to the camp's receiving center where they were quickly fed, issued green fatigues and shown their sleeping arrangements. Then it was promptly "lights out!" clearly telling everyone that you were no longer in control of anything, all decisions from here on out were being made by someone else. "Welcome to boot camp, guys! As if you hadn't already guessed, you are hereby informed: You'll never get rich by digging a ditch, you stupid son-of-a-bitch! You're in the Army now!"

The next day, Milton and his new buddies were all unceremoniously awakened at four in the morning, ordered to quickly dress and rush outside and stand in rigid, unbending formation. These young men, of course unable to see anything, wondered what the hell could be coming next, as various sergeants, like vicious dogs, milled about them, swearing and barking and snapping out commands to no one in particular and everyone in general. Not only was he offended, Milton was shocked, having no idea this kind of treatment was possible. If this were the South Vietnamese Army, he could certainly have believed it, but not the Army of the impeccably uniformed officers he knew in Saigon. Just what in this crazy world was going on?

For over an hour they stood in silent attention, literally

afraid to move as the sergeants paraded in front of them, tossing insults, berating individual soldiers, assigning nicknames, daring anyone to laugh or whimper, all this an early morning wake-up call to the Army's true intent, an unyielding introduction to a new reality intended to knock you down and stand you up upon your head. One mean-looking sergeant, shopping for victims, stopped at Milton, asking his name then interrupting, cutting him off with a terse, "No! You're wrong! Your name is Shithead! In fact, all of you are shitheads!" he shouted, wanting everyone to know beyond any doubt just how the Army felt about them. It was a wonderful start to a pleasant experience. At least it was unforgettable. Milton certainly never forgot it.

After this bit of extemporaneous theater, no applause necessary please, they were marched off to breakfast. Then came more physicals, inoculations, and finally, that pivotal dehumanizing ritual, the obligatory buzz cut, shedding not only hair but your civilian individuality and identity as well, making it clear, plain as day, as if you didn't already know, you were now an involuntary participant in a unique lifestyle, where obedience was everything, and defiance, more than just blasphemy, was dangerous subversion, never to be tolerated. Aren't you glad and proud to be in the Army now?

As I've said, Milton truly didn't know what he had gotten himself into, having given no thought about the strength and stamina required to pass the Army's basic training. At least physically, he was completely unprepared for the relentless series of arduous, non-stop drilling and training, not understanding that they were preparing him to fight a war, not to live out a personal daydream played out on an imaginary beach. He immediately fell behind, failing to progress to the drill instructor's expectations. The forced marches and running from station to station were evidently more vigorous than waiting tables. He simply couldn't keep up.

As mornings were generally reserved for physical activities, afternoons were slated for more leisurely training and propaganda films, lectures and verbal presentations concerning military codes, and why, if you just so happened to be shipped over to South Vietnam, your death might be necessary. The Army wanted to keep things clear, all regulations and rules and expectations thoroughly known and respected. That was the Army way, precise, to the point, minus any hidden agendas.

Fort Lewis' auditoriums and lecture halls were stifling, poorly ventilated places, overcrowded and brutally warm, making every talk an ordeal to remain alert, let alone trying to stay awake listening to something you never wanted to hear, nothing you would ever seriously remember. Unfortunately, no allowances were made for napping. The morning's rigorous drills, acting in combination with the heat generated by so many young bodies, naturally led to dozing off. The unsuspecting dreaming recruits would suddenly be rudely awakened by a sharp rap to the head delivered by billy club wielding MPs patrolling the aisles. The Army wanted to make sure everyone was paying attention. I'm sure on some level they were. It was very difficult if not impossible to miss what the Army was saying, not that many were inclined to hear it.

As the first few weeks progressed, Milton's performance continued to decline to the point that he was actually missing meals. A time-honored Fort Lewis tradition required that recruits run an extensive obstacle course before all mess hall calls, maybe thinking it built up a soldierly appetite. But alas, for poor Milton it meant near starvation as he repeatedly failed to reach the mess halls before the doors closed. He just didn't have the upper body strength to get through it, Milton dangling from the parallel bars like a solitary leaf in the wind. Initially seen as comic, the sergeants stopped laughing after Milton's chronic failure became habitual, an everyday occurrence. He may not have sensed it, but he was on the verge of flunking boot camp, qualifying himself for that ultimate Army insult: the general discharge, total disgrace hidden within bureaucratic euphemism.

Because the drill sergeants were graded, holding personal accountability for a recruit's failure or success, there was a strong incentive to get guys like Milton through this most elemental of army training. In military terms, this was kindergarten stuff, barely out of the sandbox. If Milton couldn't hack this, the answer was obvious, the Army couldn't use him and he would have to leave. His only glimmer of hope was his continually expressed optimism. He wanted to be a soldier, Milton both fitting yet breaking the mold. If a route existed to help him succeed, his sergeants were interested in finding it. Though as fate would have it, circumstances suddenly intervened, sending everyone involved the clear message that the situation had better quickly change or Milton would accidentally kill himself.

The presiding drill sergeant should have known better, and after Milton injured himself, they all must have remarked that they had seen this coming. Some brilliant individual assigned Milton the task of providing "cover fire" during a live ammunition drill, theoretically providing actual combat experience with no loss of life or limb. In this case, providing cover meant giving Milton a real rifle with actual bullets and expecting him to fire it safely. Remember, this is the same soldier who couldn't make it to the chow line on time, even with a head start. Somebody was either overly optimistic or drunk.

Firing lines are noisy places, certainly not for the timid, not with a constant popping of carbines and the staccato rattling of automatic rifles and machine guns all combining their murderous voices into a screaming metallic chorus chiming and pinging a deadly hallelujah. It was directly into the middle of this chaotic din the unfortunate Milton was hopefully inserted, poised to provide a stream of live bullets protecting his buddies attacking the enemy during an imaginary fire fight. Who knows how well trained he was in the use of weapons before being handed his M-14 automatic rifle, one of the many types of guns used in the jungles and high plateaus of South Vietnam. Given what occurred next, whatever instruction he had attended, he must have slept through most of it.

So try to picture the situation. Here is the inadequately trained Milton, thoroughly distracted by the roaring gunfire, M-14 tightly in hand, completely frozen, unable to move let alone pull a trigger. Seeing his hesitation, the sergeant yells at him to begin firing, what the hell did he think he was doing anyway, prompting Milton to sharply bring up his rifle, not to his shoulder but to his face, squarely pressing the rifle butt against his nose and mouth and firing, the recoil instantly knocking out two front teeth, his mouth suddenly a crimson mess, blood streaming down his face, soiling his nice, fresh fatigues.

The sergeant screamed at everyone to cease firing, as shocked as Milton at what had just happened. It wasn't considered a general or commonplace procedure placing a rifle to your nose, Milton's training manual obviously containing a serious misprint. None of the sergeants could believe what he had done, something literally beyond their imagination.

Evidently, Milton's accident was a definite first, a kind of almost humorous milestone for Fort Lewis; and a very singular example of how not to properly handle a rifle during any and all conditions. Milton quickly became a minor celebrity, developing the reputation as someone completely out of his element. If he hadn't kept repeating how much he wanted to be a soldier, he would have been given his discharge right then and there, just to keep him from killing himself. But if he wanted to be soldier, they would do their best to make him one. Given that nearly everyone else didn't want to be there, it was refreshing to discover someone who actually did.

To save Milton, and probably everyone else within his general proximity, he was transferred to a special training platoon, a kind of remedial boot camp, the Modern Army's version of primary school. This unit was a much safer playground, with fewer sharp objects, coming with the small request, that if at all possible, could you please refrain from eating the crayons. Even though Milton knew this represented his last chance to be a soldier, he couldn't help feeling disappointed and a little sorry for himself, embarrassed that he was now classified as part of a very distinctive, dysfunctional crowd. That he too was also a misfit amongst miscreants, suddenly crowned emperor of the dung hill. And be sure he didn't like it. No, no, not at all. It was all too depressing. What had he done to deserve this ignominious treatment? He felt he was doing the best he could. Yet somehow it just wasn't good enough. Frustration was now his new middle name.

Fort Lewis' "special needs" unit, tucked away in a faraway corner of that sprawling base, was the Army's response to an obvious problem created by a wartime draft conscripting any and all males between the ages 18 and 26: you were going to pick up a few oddballs along the way. Though out of shape, at least Milton was on the correct side of normal, deemed reasonably sane. That couldn't be said about the majority of those assigned to this particular unit. How these guys slipped through the pre-induction process, the sergeants could only guess. The developmentally disabled, the mentally ill, the sociopaths were all there in their confused and demented glory, human conundrums waiting to be deciphered and molded into soldiers. It was an immense, sometimes complex undertaking.

Few, if any of the sergeants had ever received any formal psychiatric training, but of course that didn't stop the Army from daily delivering up a variety of schizophrenics, manic-depressives and your commonplace, everyday neurotic upon their doorstep. It might have been a menagerie but a gentle one, a new kind of petting zoo for the feral and poorly domesticated. Just because you were half-cracked or illiterate didn't necessarily mean that "Today's Army" had no use for you.

To the contrary, as long as you weren't actively hallucinating or convulsing, you could always peel potatoes or mop the barracks floor. The Army had many areas of expertise, and certainly something suitable could be found for you. At least that's what the sergeants hoped and prayed for while mending the psyche and soothing the anguished soul of their new wards. Given that this was their last opportunity to mend the broken recruit, the sergeants involved were highly motivated, minor miracle workers transforming flawed civilians into functional soldiers, at least capable of sweeping a warehouse, if not firing a gun in anger.

Milton's brief vacation from ordinary boot camp was just what he needed, a respite from his own anxiety. It was immediately clear that there was nothing seriously wrong. He just needed a slower pace, that's all, not much else, Milton having quickly gained the reputation as a lamb amongst wolves, just a good guy wanting to go back home, home in this case being South Vietnam. That Milton still didn't consider Seattle home spoke much concerning his current psychology, his internal dilemma, constantly telling anyone who would listen how much he missed Saigon and his parents. Milton couldn't have picked a more sympathetic theme, everyone at Fort Lewis missing home and dreading an uncertain future.

Nobody truly wanted to be there, everyone having that in common, anywhere but Fort Lewis. For Milton it was Saigon. For others it was west Texas or upstate New York or some other corner of the good old USA. It was not an issue of where your home was, home simply was home, with everyone sharing his or her version of Milton's wish, a sad smile upon a gray Northwest day, those damn clouds obscuring the brightest notions. Who cared about today? Next year, two years from now being important, nothing else, just getting through all this, locking the door and walking away intact, back with friends and the wife and kids. That was it, the only story anyone cared about. To hell with everything else, none of it mattering. As the general sentiment went, the Army could all damn well go screw itself, the faster the better.

After two weeks, Milton returned to regular boot camp

revitalized and rejuvenated and transformed—even prepared to reach chow on time and perhaps staying awake during those boring lectures. And maybe, just maybe, even occasionally firing a rifle but then again, maybe not, the Army probably feeling it was better to be safe rather than extremely sorry, better not to push him into being another Sergeant York. Besides, Milton didn't look anything like Gary Cooper. He was too short and definitely was not from Tennessee.

Since he faced nearly two more years in the army, the best result of his ten weeks in boot camp certainly wasn't that he became an actual soldier. No, something far more important occurred. Instead he became someone very different, a kind of company mascot, pleasant to have around, an all-around good buddy and compatriot.

Though initially sounding negative, that he somehow wasn't taken seriously, it meant exactly the opposite. Instead it was a true recognition of what and who he actually was: an innocent civilian caught up by conscription, never to be identified as a pretend soldier ready to fight in a real war. His sergeants understood he would never be that, and that was perfectly okay. It wasn't necessary. He was too vulnerable, not wise putting someone like him on the frontlines. Better for him and better for everyone concerned to keep Milton as far away as possible from real weapons, no one forgetting that day on the firing line. No point or reason in getting anyone hurt. It served no functional purpose to have him do something he wasn't capable of. Let him coast through his two years in the Army and be done with it. There was no harm in that. And certainly a much safer policy than the alternative, Milton not yet ready for dentures.

These attitudes ultimately proved extremely advantageous, following Milton from boot camp throughout his entire Army career, repeatedly receiving safe assignments regardless of where he went. It was as if a warning had been placed in his service files, and perhaps it was written somewhere, admonishing everyone to keep watch, to make sure he didn't get into any serious trouble. Given Milton's language skills, reasonably conversant in Cantonese, Mandarin, Vietnamese and English, one would think the Army would have made him an interpreter, immediately shipping him off to the front lines. Logic would have indicated that—but like I said, happily for Milton, it never happened.

After graduating from boot camp, Milton entered a kind of official purgatory, a nebulous period of endless anxiety, as he and all the other newly manufactured soldiers waited for their permanent assignments. Other than Milton of course, no one wanted to go to South Vietnam. With hundreds of Americans now dying weekly, it didn't seem like the most opportune destination. Anywhere but South Vietnam was the common sentiment. Tempers were understandably short, now that there was nothing to do except wait. A heightened sensitivity, a new tension took over the barracks. Fistfights, especially between the black and white soldiers, broke out daily. Urban, northern blacks found themselves sharing bunks with rural, southern whites. Conflicts, however minor they might be, were inevitable.

The basic conscripted soldier's position was simple. He was in the Army involuntarily and now he was going somewhere he didn't want to go, and do something he didn't want to do. Kiss his hometown sweetheart, maybe, but certainly not to be assigned to South Vietnam and kill or be killed. It was illogical and stupid. And whether it was or wasn't, they were now all entered into the most important lottery of their young lives. If you were lucky, West Germany or South Korea would be the draw. Michael Wan for one was very fortunate, shipped off to Fort Campbell, Kentucky, for his two entire years. You know where the losers went. It just didn't seem fair, or again, logical. My own brother Steve, also drafted in 1967, despite earning a sniper medal in boot camp and having shot moose and ducks in Alaska, was sent off to Germany to drive trucks. Doesn't a good shooter, someone experienced firing a rifle, belong on the battlefront? According to the United States Army, that was evidently not the case. Army logic turned left when the opposite direction was called for. Why not drive directly into a ditch? We will tow you out in the morning and treat it like a training exercise, everyone benefiting from the experience.

Speaking of appropriate and especially lucky, Milton, after a nearly three-week wait, was informed that the best use of his unique skills would be to remain at Fort Lewis and do the laundry, washing clothes his ideal military assignment. Maybe it had something to do with there once being a Chinese laundry located on every corner in the larger American cities. Or another prime example of Army logic at its theoretical best, simple answers for complex equations.

Regardless of the rationale involved, he had definitely won a prime appointment, remaining safely bound to American soil. His fellow suffers couldn't believe it, and neither could Milton, who of course now felt extremely disappointed. This wasn't part of his master plan.

Instead of South Vietnam, Milton's new assignment was the quartermaster unit of the 239th Infantry Company, Fort Lewis, Washington. The Army had to have clean uniforms; there was no avoiding that necessity. Where would "Today's Military" be without properly cleaned and pressed trousers? I know it's impossible to imagine an Army minus all the regulations, and heaven forbid, clean uniforms.

I suppose you could do worse, conscripted to battle dirt and grime, dirt certainly an unrelenting and tenacious foe, never known to back down from a fight. Milton would now be taught the finer points of washing clothes under even the most difficult conditions.

Soldiers and their uniforms are intrinsically linked, the uniform separating the modern warrior in time from the primitive, nearly naked, unwashed hordes that battled each other clad merely in deer skins and bear hides. In those distant days, soldierly garments, along with the men wearing them of course, were considered fairly disposable. Always a multitude of wild animals available to be hunted and fresh skins taken, readily transformed into the most fashionable of battle wear.

Milton's modern Army maintained a different philosophy, relative economy, at least for the common soldier, was considered tantamount, a set of fatigues expected to last an entire two years' service. This meant proper care, meaning the efficient washing and drying of all those valuable uniforms. And when the soldiers were done with them, the used garments were sold to the local Army & Navy surplus stores and outlets, guaranteeing the clothes a second life plus a small additional profit for the government.

All this distilled wisdom was translated down to Milton, the man chosen to maintain the Army's standards and traditions. When again sitting in those darkened theaters viewing the glory of men in combat, please give a few seconds thought to Milton and the men and women like him laboring to provide all those impeccably clean uniforms blown up in Technicolor upon the silver screen. You don't think John Wayne did his own laundry, do you? Not a chance! Also be sure to add Mel Gibson and the other assorted heroes to that hygienic tradition. Mercy! Where would they all be without their clean wardrobes? Why it could even cost them an Academy Award nomination. We can't let that happen.

Other than transferring to different barracks, Milton's transition couldn't have been smoother. After a couple weeks orientation, he was ready to wash clothes Army-style. His favorite training exercise had to be the high-volume washing during simulated battlefield conditions, using what can best be described as a laundry truck—an immense self-contained laundromat on wheels, carrying huge washers and dryers, their capacities measured in cubic yards. His unit practiced at lakesides and rivers; pumping fresh water through large hoses as wide as Milton was tall into the gigantic, thirsty machines. He had never imagined anything like this, akin to watching a family of giants in a fairy tale washing their clothes assisted by a troop of dwarves. Unfortunately, Milton didn't find his permanent assignment nearly as exciting or magical.

Milton's new placement, his Army home away from home, was the base laundromat. No, I don't mean the kind you're probably familiar with—dirty, boxy, rectangle-shaped rooms filled with coin-operated machines and sweating mothers harried by restless gangs of noisy children. No, instead this laundromat was a clothes-washing factory situated in a large, sprawling warehouse taking up an entire square block, a world within a world utilizing hundreds of workers on assembly lines sorting, labeling and pressing tens of thousands of assorted garments daily.

Matching the importance of the mess halls, Fort Lewis could not have functioned without it. The soldiers had to have clean uniforms. Call it the sanitary nerve center of the entire base. If the laundry stopped operating, within days mountains of dirty fatigues and undershirts would have overwhelmed the base, impeding daily operations. You can imagine how unacceptable it would be having your modern legions marching off to do battle in dirty socks. Even recently I read an article in the local Tacoma, Washington daily praising the efforts of a local quartermaster unit newly returned from the Iraq War, doing just what I have described. New weapons systems may come and go but clean uniforms will always be at the core of any military success.

Surprisingly, Milton and his fellow soldiers working the laundry detail fell under the direct supervision of a team of civilian women who held complete responsibility for the daily operations. These civilians issued the orders and Milton and his cohorts obeyed. It really wasn't a bad arrangement, working out for everyone, much easier than dealing with a barking sergeant. Though not particularly prestigious, the job had few inherent negatives other than the wilting heat and unceasing cacophony generated by the washing machines. It might have been a kind of hell but certainly a minor one, the soldiers grateful to be stationed at Fort Lewis and out of harm's—if not grime's—way. It was essentially impossible to get killed washing fatigues unless you purposely climbed into one of the machines, shutting the door behind you.

For the laundry matrons, it was a good arrangement. They got a decent wage and had a responsive team of cooperative workers. And if anyone had to be disciplined, the Army handled it, not them. Life was good in this insular environment called Fort Lewis, a controlled chemistry lab with all the experiments safe and predictable, no exploding test tubes and genetically altered rats chewing through the insulation.

Other than a three-month-long transfer to nearby Madigan General Hospital to have his teeth worked on, you now know what Milton's primary duties were during his first year and a half of military service. Sure, there was the predictable "policing" of the mess hall grounds after meals and random guard duty marching round and round a truck parked in the middle of nowhere. But other than these kinds of minor irritants, he had few complaints. His only real objection was the daily marching in formation to and from the laundry, which seemed silly, which it probably was. It wasn't like they were preparing for mortal combat. Milton was now obviously spoiled, given that his overall routine was nearly devoid of military ritual and order. Life was fat and I'm just not making reference to the army chow. He was having a reasonable if not always good time.

Milton's weekends were now devoid of military obligations, other than having to be back for muster on Monday mornings. On Friday afternoons, he would hop in his big, white Oldsmobile 442 convertible, having earlier discarded his faithful Desoto, and take off for Seattle to visit his family or shoot down to Chinatown to test his luck. Occasionally he went on excursions with his friends Tam and Woo, two Chinese buddies from the laundry, going north to Vancouver, British Columbia, Canada, or down south to Portland, Oregon. Other than never having enough money, Milton was more or less enjoying himself.

How could he really find complaint? He still chaffed his sergeants about returning to South Vietnam, but was told that instead he was heading off to Washington, D.C. to personally guard the president. Sometimes Milton resented being treated like a living, breathing comic book Sad Sack or Beetle Bailey, but it wasn't like he was doing permanent KP (kitchen patrol) duty, washing dishes and peeling potatoes. He was on a government holiday and he knew it. If the scenery was a trifle monotonous, what of it, at least it wasn't the steaming jungle. At least there was towering Mount Rainier looming in all its magnificence over the camp, a friendly volcano saying hello on the rare sunny and cloudless days.

After a year of soap and suds, Milton was purposely transferred to the dental offices centered in Madigan General Hospital to accommodate his dental work. It was definitely a mission of empathy and convenience, Milton getting his teeth worked on when he wasn't sweeping the floors or filing papers. Milton's mouth was a dentist's nightmare, the teeth missing from his accident only the beginning of his problems. He remained as the dentist's assistant and primary patient for three months, and then it was back to the bustle and swelter of the laundry. If he did go to Vietnam, now at least he wouldn't have many toothaches as long as he brushed his teeth.

Upon his return, Milton found himself promoted to acting corporal, a totally unexpected but very friendly gesture, a signal that he was about to have his foremost wish granted. With only nine months of service left, it would have to happen quickly, or not at all. Life was very pleasant for him at Fort Lewis. He was now tutoring various officers in Vietnamese. Except for the forty total hours required at the laundry, his time was his own. He was free to do what he wanted. Obviously, he didn't have to leave, instead peacefully closing out his service, but if he wanted to go to South Vietnam, why not? It was his home. And didn't he say he still had a girlfriend there? Other than the danger, he might as well go, and good luck to him, too!

Finally, to Milton's profound relief, he received his orders for South Vietnam. He found that he was scheduled to leave for Saigon in early November 1968. As a kind of going away present, he was nominated for promotion to sergeant, but only given one, very short week to prepare for his oral presentation.

All of this, his orders for Vietnam, his potential promotion, was all evidence of Milton's widespread popularity. I'm sure his friends thought, knowing how the Army works, that he would be safer over there as a sergeant. Was he really qualified to be a sergeant? Probably not, but where was the harm in trying? You never knew what the Army would say nor do one way or the bloody other.

Milton's presentation started poorly enough by his inexplicable failure to salute the sitting panel of examiners—obviously not understanding the finer points of military protocol, dooming all hopes for any positive outcomes. Of course he wasn't a soldier. He was just an innocent, good-natured young man who just happened to be wearing a uniform, almost like someone attending a costume party, pretending to be a bona fide soldier.

The examiners certainly understood this and weren't in any mood to encourage this kind of nonsense. To begin with, they didn't trust draftees, feeling that all these reluctant civilians made the poorest soldiers. Not only did they think Milton was unqualified, they felt it was potentially dangerous having someone like him issuing orders in an active war zone. What were his superiors thinking, recommending him for a promotion? Were they out of their minds? Not only were the panel members unfriendly, they were discouraging, making it clear what their final decision would be. Milton saw clearly he would never be a sergeant. Like the hearings in Hong Kong, he just wanted this to be over. He had his orders for South Vietnam. That was enough.

Milton realized that there were two extremely distinct

United States Armies: the official Army, the one presented to the American public, the paper-driven, spit-and-polish, by-the-code-book Army; the Army represented by the officers that he first seen and feared in Saigon. The other was the authentic Army that he knew from boot camp and beyond, the actual Army that did the fighting and dying. This was the Army that wrote to a dead buddies' wife, the Army that could give a damn about official regulations, only interested in getting the job done without a bunch of jawing and analysis and brass hats screwing up the process. After eighteen months he understood well enough that the Army he cared for was all about mutual camaraderie, respect and friendship. It was that Army that had given him his new teeth, that Army sending him back to Saigon. He found he had no interest in the official Army. The sentiment was mutual, Milton only a cog in the great, green washing machine. Milton had friends where it really counted, in the real Army, and that was good enough for him.

His friends were less than pleased that his promotion had been rejected. His sergeant major, profanely describing what he really thought about the Army brass, told Milton to keep wearing his corporal stripes anyway. Maybe he would somehow get to keep them. Anything in theory was possible, because as I said a couple paragraphs back, one just never knew what the Army, in its profound wisdom would do. Why he just might come back as a heralded four-star general riding a donkey fanned by palm fronds upon reentering the gates of Fort Lewis.

It appeared that truly anything was possible, even being assigned to South Vietnam as a personal favor while Americans were now dying out there at a rate of two thousand or more month after terrible month. That made for a lot of grieving families. Especially since the January-February 1968 Tet Offensive, the war had accelerated to a new, deadlier pace. South Vietnam was now an active battlefield better left to someone else. Milton instead was about to embrace it, the lost son reaching for his elusive father.

In preparation for his return, Milton was excused from any further laundry duty and given a couple of weeks off to get his personal affairs together. He had written his mother about his pending return hoping, now that she owned a restaurant catering to American soldiers, she could somehow assist with getting him assigned somewhere near or in Saigon.

From the beginning of all this, he envisioned himself returning to Saigon and having a heartwarming reunion with his parents. Logically then, the conclusion to this personal sojourn had to be Saigon. Milton, ever the amateur gambler, was playing the odds. Otherwise, he would have been much better off remaining at the laundry. His only guarantee now was that he would be based somewhere in South Vietnam. Sometimes he truly wondered why he was returning, but it was far too late now for any final hesitation or regrets. He was going so he might as well enjoy himself regardless of where he found himself, be it Da Nang or Hue or even floating somewhere on the Mekong River. He had asked for this. His fervent wish and desire had been granted.

On a cloudy November day, Milton left from Tacoma, Washington's McCord Air Force base, and after two layovers, and two days of solid flying, landed back near Saigon, his circular four-year journey nearly complete. As the jet landed, Milton saw a Vietnamese farmer tending his rice paddies, wearing the conical hat traditional to Vietnam. Seattle suddenly was a distant memory. Milton without question was back at home.

Some typical GIs roughhousing at the 3rd Field Hospital, pushing and shoving war's obvious realities into the background, away from conscious thought.

The newly arrived Milton, back in Saigon and chumming with the secretary at his clerical assignment.

Eight

Back in Saigon & Bigmon's Fiefdom

Superficially, viewed from a roaring jetliner, South Vietnam might have looked the same to Milton as when he left back in 1964, but it wasn't, and never would be, the country and the war having gone through dramatic, wrenching changes. Rice farming, having a timeless quality, maybe remaining what it was but the rest of South Vietnamese culture was undeniably altered, literally and figuratively blown upside down. At that moment in November 1968, the American presence was everywhere, over 600,000 soldiers and support personnel scattered throughout the country, but in a mere seven-year span, by May 1975, all of them would be gone. Gone but certainly not forgotten. The Tet Offensive had irrevocably altered the entire tenor of the war by bringing it directly to the Americans, shoving it right in their faces, the clear message being they could not hide anywhere, not in the fortressed cities or their embassy compound.

Though suffering over ten thousand killed in a handful of days, the Viet Cong and their North Vietnamese allies had made the clear statement that they were not close to being defeated, as some Americans thought. But instead it was quite evident that the only path to a complete and total victory would be the annihilation of every man, woman, child, dog

119

and cat because this enemy would never back down. Given the enemy's nearly maniacal determination, this was a very reasonable and logical surmise.

It had also become apparent that neither the United States government nor the American public was ready to sacrifice the hundreds of thousands of young men that would be necessary to bring the enemy into final submission. Many were also questioning just why the Americans were attempting to prop up a South Vietnamese government, which was at its very best benignly corrupt, and at its worst, immoral and crooked. Someone once said something to the effect that they may be bastards but at least they are our bastards. Certainly an honest and accurate assessment, given the questionable legitimacy of the South Vietnamese government the Americans were fighting to support and uphold. You might also remember that this was the same government that the CIA had helped install just five years before.

Anyway, the Americans would soon be relinquishing ownership of this entire messy affair but unfortunately, not for a few additional bloody, war-scarred years. President Nixon, that living relic of the 1950s Red Scare, first had to get his eager hands into the mix, never before having a real war at his personal command—acting like an excited child in charge of his own sandbox army. Battling real flesh and blood Communists had to be far more tangible and satisfying than chasing pink shadows lurking in liberal closets and hallways. Besides, he didn't have to share either the glory or the headlines with that bombastic fool from Wisconsin, the late Senator Joseph McCarthy.

Yes, it can accurately be said that Milton had returned to a radically different Vietnam, where thousands of Vietnamese, regardless of ideology, were dying weekly, either killed by the Americans or worse, by each other. Civil wars have never been particularly nice, usually extremely messy conflicts, ripping large holes in the cultural fabric, requiring many successive generations to mend the nearly irreparable gashes.

By taking up the political baton from the French and running with it, the United States made both Vietnams pay an exorbitant environmental, economic and human cost, a sum total certainly not matched by any perceived gain. Sadly, it was all for nothing, only delaying the obvious and inevitable.

Any reasonable gauging of nationalistic and political history would have told anyone involved and interested the final story and result. Sometimes it takes centuries but ultimately, the occupiers lose and the once enslaved emerge free and victorious. It's almost as if a natural moral law comes into play when one social group attempts to force its will upon another. All the United States had to do was look to its own war of independence against the British monarchy as its own and best example. A prime twentieth-century example is Nazi Germany's failed oppression of the European continent. There has always been something politically ugly about the forced occupation of a people and country. It is something beyond everyday tolerance. Everyone wants to be free.

Some current examples clearly display that. China's continued occupation of Tibet remains a persistent blemish. Another sorry case is Morocco's insistence that Western Sahara can never be an independent nation, solely interested in exploiting its vast mineral resources, disregarding the wishes of the resident population. Historically, every belligerent country has had its smug justifications for doing what it did, but in the end, freedom has been the final response—be it decades or centuries in the making.

Again, there appears to be an inherent morality ultimately commenting upon all human foolishness. Some will call it karma. Others would simply term it as common sense, just what is most obvious. Whatever it is, I wish everyone would understand that hurting others will never be acceptable, with the real possibility that the unknown universe is against you, so the sooner you begin acting humanely, so much the better for all concerned.

Milton's civilian charter landed at Bien Hoa airfield, a few miles outside of Saigon. Then in a rite of passage shared by all incoming Americans, he rode a bus to the Long Bien Processing Center, also home to a military detention center appropriately nicknamed the LBJ, in honor of the president so personally responsible for their visit to this once-obscure corner of the globe. Milton's first official act was to promptly fall asleep, justifiably exhausted after his long journey.

Milton felt the morning muster began somewhat oddly, as he was questioned as to why he hadn't responded to the previous day's roll-call. Late or not, though, there was certainly some very good news coming his way.

Instead of the deepest jungle battlefield, Milton found himself assigned to the Third Field Hospital, part of the 44th Medical Brigade located on the city of Saigon's outer perimeter, adjacent to a major airfield called Tan Son Nhut. Incredibly, Milton had again gained the cushy assignment, meeting all his imagined needs and requirements. He would be living in Saigon and be able do whatever he wanted. He had received his miracle.

For a mere acting corporal, he certainly seemed to hold considerable sway, influencing the mysterious machinations of military command. Now either he would have to intentionally try to get himself killed or just be extremely unlucky. It appears someone somewhere had given him a Saigon holiday. It was now up to him to enjoy it.

Milton's new home was a converted high school, a well-constructed brick building securely surrounded by a ten-foot high, razor-wire topped fence. Each corner of the hospital compound was a miniature fortress composed of sandbagged bunkers occupied by heavily armed MPs. Milton might have had one of the safest assignments in all of South Vietnam. After a few weeks, Milton even began resenting his protection after repeatedly being asked for his identification and purpose in being there. It might have been a surprise to Milton but some people actually understood that there was a war going on somewhere. A constant flow of incoming casualties did remind everyone that in an unguarded moment you too could join them. It was a sobering prospect. The war and instant death in reality was just one machine gun burst away. Enemy infiltrators freely roamed Saigon. The Tet Offensive clearly pointed that out. Milton would have known if he had read the local Seattle and Tacoma newspapers before his arrival. Or having watched Walter Cronkite's sober newscast and his dire assessment of the war, foretelling what was now obvious. But being back in Saigon should have been evidence enough. The South Vietnamese were losing the war.

Though reserved primarily for the American wounded, the hospital also had its share of Australians, South Koreans, and sometimes Vietnamese from both sides of the conflict. Occasionally, Milton would be called in to translate, finding himself face to face with the fabled enemy. Except for all the bandages, they looked like anyone you would find on the streets of Saigon. For the hospital staff of course, patients were patients, all victims of a crazy, distorted war. They didn't have time for judgments—there was surgery to perform and another life to save, polemics having nothing to do with it.

There were 120 beds to accommodate the unending river of broken and bullet- pierced young men, with a staff of nearly 100 physicians and nurses and orderlies ready 24 hours a day to receive and comfort them. Once the patient was stabilized, he was quickly evacuated to someplace even safer like Hawaii or the Philippines. The staff was there to stop the initial bleeding, to literally stop this premature hemorrhaging of an entire generation. It was neither a pleasant nor easy mission.

More than just a hospital, the Third Field facility was actually a self-contained city in miniature, containing its own generators, dining hall, PX and barracks. All the personnel shared a large entertainment center and hall called the HUB, providing a stage for the ever popular USO tours, Milton even getting his picture taken with the famed Gypsy Rose Lee—somehow I'm sure making all his travails worthwhile. If not for all the suffering and dying associated with it, the hospital might have seemed a positively benign environment. Though never quite that, it nevertheless was a good place for Milton, a personal safe haven muting some of the war's harsher realities.

Before starting his new duties as a filing clerk, he was allowed to visit his parents, everyone sympathetic to Milton's unique situation. It is interesting how Milton's abridged version of his life story trailed behind him like banners flapping in the wind, signaling a very personal SOS. This made him difficult if not impossible to ignore. I believe it's why I also decided to take up his story in the first place, a compelling emotionalism asking for company. Back in 1968, Milton's distress must have held a powerful immediacy eliciting empathy, which as I've been describing, opened various paths of opportunity. I think, without exaggeration, Milton was an exposed heart seeking solace. If that isn't compelling, I don't know what else it could be.

Now, drum rolls, please, is the part of Milton's story I hope you've been long waiting for: his much anticipated encounter with his father. He felt he had to see Wainam before anything else, ready for some kind of conclusion if not an end to their life-long estrangement. Milton was scared, obviously not knowing how his father would respond. Since leaving South Vietnam, neither Milton nor Michael had heard anything from him. Not a letter or a telephone call during the ensuing four years. For Milton, his return was highly problematic, a huge emotional gamble, but something without question he had to do.

As it turned out, their first meeting in over four years was decidedly anticlimactic. Upon arriving back at Ky Con Street, Milton found his father entertaining an American Army officer over some business matter. He was respectfully introduced as his son and that was the end of it. Milton stayed overnight, and to his complete delight, a maid personally delivered his breakfast, a maybe subtle but clear sign of a newfound acceptance, if not palpable affection. As I've repeatedly said, the Wans generally were a family of few words and outward emotions, but Milton clearly understood that something had changed. Whether large or small, he finally felt some vindication, his role as family pariah having ended, his burden suddenly lifted off and away. In any real sense, Milton had come back to Saigon to start over, to walk out the front door of the flat as an adult, leaving the bewildered child behind. His father's blessings, however subtle, changed everything, a final benison propelling him out of the door.

After receiving his father's approval, all that was left to do was visit his mother. After that he would be ready to leave, ready again for the safe confines of the laundry. Having received his father's absolution, there was little to nothing left to be achieved. Unfortunately, he still owed the Army nearly six additional months. Well, life wasn't perfect. He would have to make the best of it. And keep a low profile; Ding of course being the last man on earth he wanted to encounter. For Milton, the Viet Cong and Ding were one and the same, and in his mind, equally lethal. Trouble was something to be permanently avoided, potentially spoiling his vacation with a few irritating bullet holes.

Seeing his mother again held none of the latent anxiety connected with his father. Olga's assistance with his visas and airline tickets and everything else had firmly reestablished the bond between mother and meandering son. She was doing quite well for herself, thank you, running her own restaurant and nightclub, offering wayward American soldiers a bit of home. Consequently, her place was usually packed with young men seeking memories and hamburgers. Milton ended up eating most of his meals there, on the house of course, returning her kindness by buying discounted cases of mustard and catsup and other such delicacies vital to the American palate at the Army commissary.

Though it was his father that drew him back to South Vietnam, it was ultimately his mother's presence sustaining him during his stay. Milton saw his father on four more occasions. His mother he saw nearly every day. Despite the many hours taken up with Army business, these six months would prove to be the most intimate he ever experienced with them. At least there was one reasonably happy conscript in Saigon, and now I bet you'll start believing in fairy tales again, as sometimes they sort of do come true.

Milton's career as a shuffler of medical records ended abruptly, finding that detailed organization was a foreign science. Adding further insult was the sudden disappearance of his corporal stripes, having been demoted back to Private First Class. He was only an acting corporal anyway, and I'm sure somebody found his performance unconvincing. He certainly missed all his friends back at Fort Lewis. They were all so much nicer.

Though in hindsight, it was for the best, otherwise Milton may had never discovered how the "Real United States Army" operated if not for his transfer to Sergeant Bigmon's supply office and depot, definitely poorer for missing the experience. To better understand a character like Bigmon, I recommend reading James Jones' 1951 novel concerning army life, *From Here to Eternity*, Sergeant Bigmon the exact opposite of what the Army advertised itself to be.

Bigmon, no first name please, could also have stepped out of a Charles Dickens novel if that venerable author had been writing in the mid twentieth century, being a complete character, an incorrigible Army lifer, what Jones calls a "thirty-year man"—a master of manipulation, a juggler of every known army code and regulation. Hospital supply was far more than his station: it was his fiefdom, his universe, his own business, Bigmon completely in charge, no one getting anything without seeing him first, though possibly making some allowance if a patient was either critically ill or dying. Bigmon was beyond corruption because he was totally corrupt, crooked as any tree branch reaching for the sunshine, always ready to turn a deal and make a buck, that almighty glorious dollar bill.

Bigmon wasn't much to look at, too much army chow followed by oceans of beer having created an unhealthy, classically nondescript body, short of stature but wide of girth. This unimpressive pedestal served as the platform for a squarish head attended by a flushed, fleshy face featuring thick lips and misshapened nose framed by thick glasses shielding bloodshot eyes, his overall florid tinting the byproduct of too much sour mash. Maybe not a walking pretty picture but somehow the royal norm, the results of generational inbreeding, Bigmon of course a lower-caste duke—with Milton now his local court jester, hopefully humoring his mirthless mentor.

Milton's job at supply was the perfect marriage of convenience. Bigmon needed someone who could make deliveries and also serve as his personal chauffeur. In return Milton received a very flexible schedule plus the added bonus of having his own personally assigned jeep. What an amazingly symbiotic arrangement, making Darwin proud. Bigmon utilized Milton's language skills and knowledge of Saigon's crazy streets to guide him on his daily prowls while attending to his various business interests. After Bigmon retired for the day, Milton was free to take his jeep anywhere he wanted, insurance and gasoline provided by the Army. Bigmon truly didn't give a damn what Milton did, as long as he was available in the mornings and early afternoon—drive all the way to Hanoi, it didn't matter to him. Just be back for morning muster.

As I've implied, Bigmon owned hospital supply. It's not that his superiors were completely oblivious to his sometimes shady practices but were tolerated and basically approved because whatever the hospital needed it got immediately, sidestepping all official channels. Bigmon and his cronies, while obviously enriching themselves, were efficient, getting things done, controlling the supply networks vital to the Army's operations throughout Saigon and elsewhere in South Vietnam. You had to have materials to work with. Bigmon provided them, and essentially folks, that was the entire story. He got it done minus the strangling red tape.

It's important to understand that this privilege just wasn't handed to Bigmon. He had earned it the old fashioned way, by starting on the proverbial bottom and working his way to the top of the non-commissioned totem pole. Bigmon joined the Army during the Korean War, so now nearly eighteen years later and working upon his second war, he knew the ropes, avoiding the obvious entanglements. Though having two left feet, he danced past the entrenched bureaucracy while building up his own personally-financed pension fund. He did it because he could. And if not Bigmon it would have been somebody else lining their pockets. Bigmon wasn't trying to a general. He was just a sergeant and that was good enough for him.

Bigmon knew the system, and for a small handling fee, he could practically get you anything materially you wanted. With nearly countless tons of supplies coming into South Vietnam daily, it was inevitable a percentage of it was lost or damaged. You just couldn't fight the averages. Bigmon just happened to be good at finding what was lost. All of us as children have chanted, "Finders, keepers, losers, weepers!" You better believe that Bigmon and his fellow sergeants weren't shedding any tears, knowing full well how much the Army actually wasted on any given day. It wasn't so much self-serving cynicism as the unadulterated truth. He did his job well. The Army had no reason to complain. He just wanted to be paid what he was worth, for his sometimes unrecognized ability, that's all, something I'm sure we all share in common. Who can argue with that?

Don't believe for a moment that Bigmon didn't try to lure Milton into his nefarious transactions. To the contrary, he did everything he could to involve Milton, including veiled threats and implied blackmail, viewing him as an invaluable asset, someone who could bridge the gap between himself and his counterparts in the South Vietnamese Army. I think Sergeant Bigmon had dreams of establishing his own empire, Bigmon a new Caesar. You can't fault a guy for dreaming, can you?

Its obvious Bigmon was no saint. Instead he was the epitome of opportunism, always looking for a new opening. When he looked at Milton, his eyes bulged out, only seeing dollar bills. Milton's refusal to cooperate drove him crazy. He wanted to sell Milton's mother everything she needed at bargain prices—but first Milton would have to show some enthusiasm.

Bigmon had felt that by working together they would have made a fortune. All of which was probably true, but Milton still felt guilty about lying to Ding, souring his potential involvement in any future marginal activities. Besides, he didn't want to embarrass his parents, not wanting to end up as an invited guest to the LBJ, negating all his reasons for returning. It just didn't seem to make any sense. He liked Bigmon but not enough to jeopardize his entire future. He wasn't going to do it.

Despite Bigmon's daily threats—now almost friendly, becoming part of how they said good morning—Milton's new life in his hometown was quickly stabilizing. His cohort in supply, Remsey, a nice guy serving his second tour, got Milton an apartment in the same building he was living in, located just outside the greater hospital compound. Given Saigon's affordability, even the average GI could live outside the bases and escape the usual Army rigmarole. Along with the jeep, having his own apartment meant more personal freedom especially since Fong was back in his life.

Milton had made a point of searching her out, luckily finding her at the same restaurant. I assume she was still married but I don't know that for sure. In various ways, Milton's life upon his return to Saigon was far more complete than it had been in Seattle, unquestionably holding an intimacy starkly missing from his life in America. Though happy he had emigrated, he at times felt profoundly lonely. That of course abruptly changed upon entering the Army. You're never alone in the Army. And now Milton had found the companionship he had missed, Fong now a part-time roommate. His buddy Remsey was also his next door neighbor. Every time the shooting got too close, something occurring with more frequency, they would huddle together with their M-14's imagining the worst, never knowing when the war would come knocking at their door.

Officially, Milton didn't have much to do. Waiting around for Bigmon wasn't a particularly strenuous activity. Mostly, he bantered with Remsey, passing the time away on slow tropical days. Occasionally the few deliveries beckoned. Once a week he would pick up the hospital's bottled water supply, abandoning his faithful jeep for a two-ton truck. He also made a few runs delivering sheets to the same BOQs he and Michael had worked in. He once even saw Ding driving by on his motor scooter. Instead of waving he ducked.

Milton's story of the returning native son was featured in the Army's Stars and Stripes newspaper. He had mixed feelings, fearing that the article would make him a prime target for the Viet Cong, never dawning on him that they probably weren't on the subscription list. Still he enjoyed the celebrity and attention, something new to him.

Far more ominous was the interest shown by the various field officers stopping by supply, inquiring if they could borrow Milton. Who would make a better interpreter? Bigmon though immediately killed all such requests, loudly protesting that Milton was just too valuable to be spared, calling him irreplaceable and indispensable. No, Milton would have to stay in supply.

As you might guess, Bigmon did demand some favors in return for his strident loyalty, something Milton certainly couldn't argue, even if he wanted to. He was at his good sergeant's mercy. The last thing he wanted to do was experience the front lines, daily noting the incoming wounded. Please, no thank you! Supply was his ultimate sanctuary and salvation. He was thankful for that. Bigmon was a bully but at least he wasn't aiming a gun at him.

All the troops serving in South Vietnam received two weeks of R & R (Rest & Relaxation) every year; evenly split into one week periods every six months. Logically then, Milton should have gotten just one R & R furlough, as opposed to the two he actually received, again maybe the result of Bigmon's benign influence. What a way to manage an army! Anyway, for his first holiday, Milton chose Taiwan, and why not, wasn't he once a citizen of that island nation?

At least during the Vietnam War, the American military had created their own currency, something they called military payment certificates, or as they were popularly known, MPCs. Theoretically they were equal to a dollar, but never becoming one until you left the country, the government then allowing an equal one for one exchange: one American greenback for each MPC received. Curiously, back in South Vietnam your one solitary dollar could be exchanged for two MPCs. It meant that a few of these exchanges would make you a very wealthy soldier, doubling your money each time you returned from R & R. It was an utterly safe gamble and completely legal if you found someone to cooperate. Bigmon knew that soldier. His name was Milton Wan.

On each of his two R & R's, the second being to Hong Kong, Milton carried $3,000 worth of Bigmon's MPCs, each time exchanging them for cash. Beyond receiving a few hard stares, no one bothered him. Upon Milton's return, Bigmon converted the cash back into MPCs, that is, $6,000. There is no telling how many times Bigmon turned this trick. What I am quite sure of was that he must have enjoyed a comfortable retirement. Every angle was Bigmon's geometry, a minor criminal in a wolf's fatigues.

To give you a more concrete idea of the profitability this kind of scheme could bring, back in 1968 you could buy a very nice car, let's say a Chevrolet, for $2,000. So after Milton's two trips abroad, Bigmon could now buy six Chevrolets, opening his own car lot. This made him a very happy and contented supply sergeant. Milton had been a good mule, with minimum kicking and braying involved. Now he could almost forgive him for being such a jackass for not becoming a business partner, taking what he got and not griping about it. $12,000 was a lot of money in 1968!

With four months gone, and roughly two to go, Milton had a slightly wild idea. Motivated by love or madness or was it both, he decided he wanted to marry Fong and take her back to Seattle. Wasn't she still married? Whatever her matrimonial status, the Army wasn't very encouraging when it came to bringing home Vietnamese brides. He sought out an Army chaplain for advice and counsel, who somehow misunderstood Milton's unique situation and background, talking to him like he was some ordinary GI fresh out of Iowa or Montana or some other such place. He stupidly gave the already bewildered lover the standard Army line concerning why such betrothals didn't work out, etcetera.

This initial discouragement unfortunately dissuaded him from following through and filing all the necessary forms. Though vowing to see it through, it was an idle promise never kept. He found the procedure too overwhelming, something he couldn't face, even for something this important. This was the first signal that Milton was heading into a mental decline.

During these final two months in South Vietnam, Milton lapsed into a sudden deterioration, a depression that sometimes descended into paranoia. I believe he felt extremely conflicted, now for the very first time, not wanting to leave Saigon, the reality of life in Seattle far from what he had expected. He didn't like either the uncertainty or leaving Fong behind.

He began fantasizing about his own death, not wanting to leave Saigon yet becoming deeply afraid that he would soon die if he remained, killed by the Viet Cong or Ding's associates. One incident in particular pushed him closer to a self-created brink, exaggerating an already innate inferiority, an estrangement from all home and country, the old feeling that he didn't belong anywhere or to anything, disconnected from any perceived or tangible foundation. In short, he was dispirited and morose, mimicking the happiness he had genuinely enjoyed the past four months.

Milton was driving his jeep past an ARVN base when a motor scooter with two riders suddenly darted out headlong into oncoming traffic, striking his jeep. Neither Milton nor his passenger, a young American private were injured, but the two Vietnamese soldiers, having tumbled off the scooter, were now shouting curses at Milton, yelling that it was his fault. They of course had no idea that Milton understood each and every indignant word.

A curious crowd gathered, wondering where this confrontation would lead. Milton was highly disconcerted after hearing the suggestion that he should be shot. Obviously the ARVN soldiers were not going to kill two Americans, at least not in broad daylight with hundreds of witnesses. Still, Milton was worried, telling the private to call Bigmon.

A pair of National Police officers arrived, attempting to restore a little order amidst all the shouting. Taking Milton's identification, they walked over to the offended soldiers to get their side of the incident. Milton again didn't like what he was hearing. It seemed to be entirely his fault. Milton was not appreciating the police officers' attitudes, showing too much sympathy to the soldiers' side of the story. But why worry? Wasn't Bigmon on the way?

And as quickly as it had begun it was over, as our hero and supreme patriot Sgt. Bigmon came roaring to the rescue in a big truck filled with a platoon of armed American soldiers. Have I neglected to tell you about the occasional friction between the erstwhile allies? Anyway, the animosity was real enough, which is why Bigmon came fully prepared to do battle, leaping from the truck screaming bloody murder, ripping Milton's ID away, telling everyone to go to hell, and forget that this had ever happened.

Whether any of the Vietnamese spoke English is unknown, but nevertheless they seemed to have understood Bigmon's message clearly enough. With one last glare, the ever diplomatic Bigmon and all those crazy Americans left, proving once again the efficacy of tact and negotiation. Milton drove away pleased at being rescued though feeling more anonymous than before, more than ever a stranger in his own country. He was ready to depart, his daydreaming over.

Another incident around this time added further frosting to Milton's disappointed confection. Doing the rounds with Bigmon, he entered the bar of an NCO club for a Coke, only to have the American Army sergeant in charge refuse him entry because he was armed with a service revolver. Milton's offer to take it off didn't assuage him, loudly ordering him out while the Vietnamese bargirls laughed. Nearly forty-five years later, Milton remains insulted, prepared to rip the rude sergeant into nice little pieces.

Having just one month left, Milton took that last R & R to Hong Kong, saying hello again and thanks to Auntie Wong, who was both pleased and surprised to once again encounter one of her wandering lambs. After getting back to Saigon, Milton's sense of alienation only increased, further curtailing his movements, limiting himself to his usual duties and daily visits to his mother. Milton felt vulnerable and exhausted, unwilling to take any unnecessary risks.

You might be wondering if Milton's increased caution meant that the fighting had intensified in and around Saigon. The answer is no, at least no more than was normal during that particular stage of the war. Certainly his fears held some legitimacy. The war was expanding, and clearly South Vietnam was not winning. I would say those were unavoidable conclusions. No one's safety was guaranteed. Getting killed was not a hypothetical notion. It was the prevailing reality. Milton wasn't interested in the $5,000 reenlistment bonus money the Army offered him. They couldn't give him enough dollars to stay. He had had enough of his South Vietnam adventure, feeling there was little to gain by remaining.

On their last and final meeting, Fong brought along her young son, his age matching the years they had known each other. Neither of them spoke about the boy. Milton promised he would come back for her. Certainly at the time I'm sure he meant every word but it wasn't a promise he would be able to keep. He would never see her again.

Milton said his final goodbyes, making a special effort to see his father, not knowing if he would ever see him again. Wainam smiled. They were older now, finally father and son. Milton was pleased, now having both a mother and a father. Bigmon was cheerful, kidding Milton of course, wishing him the best. There wasn't much more to say, nothing left to do. He was just another soldier returning home. It was time to go.

Being both alive and reasonably intact, Milton left Saigon and the war and the Army behind, arriving back in the United States on May 4, 1969, lucky to the end, having been discharged ten days early and still getting paid for it. He had $600. That was it, Milton remaining the big spender. He was even without a car, having sold his Oldsmobile before returning to Saigon. Though minus transportation after his Saigon visitation, Milton was now better prepared to make his life as an American, to see himself as an American and nothing else. Whether he had achieved all his expectations and dreams was unimportant, he had literally gotten everything he had asked for. Unfortunately, it wouldn't always be so easy, if all his past struggles could be termed that way.

Most of all though, he got what he wanted, what every immigrant wants: the opportunity to succeed, to freely move forward without obvious impediments and obstacles blocking his way. Life was now his for the taking, open to his personal interpretation. The circle between his two cities, Saigon and

Seattle, was now closed. He was completely on his own. It was now time to take control, because no one else could do that for him. The door to his future was wide open. It was time, without hesitation, to enter and walk through. Without question, the United States, now and forever, was his home.

Milton standing in front of "dream" deployment, the Third Field Hospital. It is now a school.

Enjoying some entertainment with his fellow conscripts.

Standing with his mother at her famous restaurant.

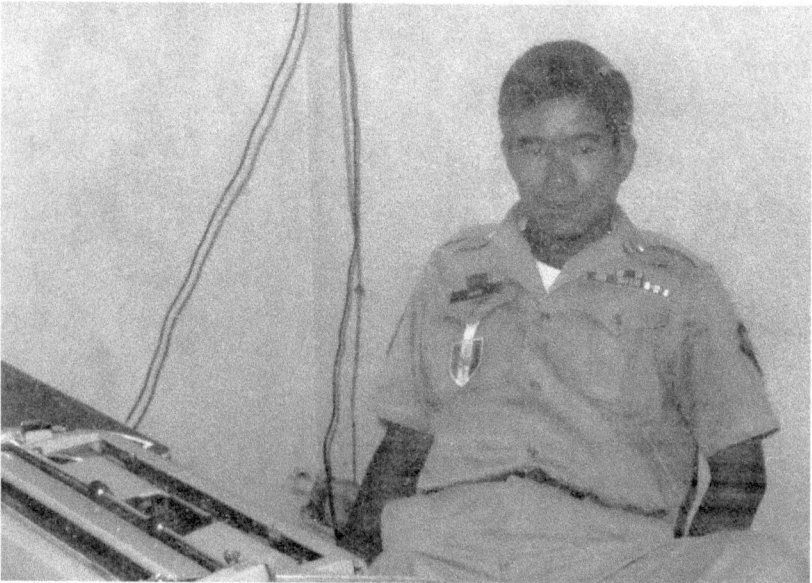

Hard at work at Bigmon's hospital supply.

EPILOGUE

You've just read a biographical story, an episode and era of Milton Wan's life that concluded nearly four decades ago, but of course his life continued, Milton remaining alive and I am happy to report, doing reasonably well as I write this. I usually see Milton nearly every weekend, working hard behind Tai Tung's front counter, doing what he knows well, quickly serving the always impatient customers. Watching him work, I wish they tipped more than the usual paltry change or solitary dollar left upon the counter. He and his cousin Jimmy definitely deserve more.

In writing his story I've been tempted more than once to bring his history up to the current date but have decided against it, comfortable with Milton's initial request to confine my examination to his earliest years. I'll leave it up to him to write the remainder of his story, as he sees fit or not. What strikes me most about the current Milton I know so well is how his entire life story lives and breathes within him. I see his father's abuse, his early childhood struggles, his frustration and confusion etched upon his face, expressed in his every physical movement. In short, he became his life. What he was many yesterdays ago is who he is today.

I believe this is an elemental truth applicable to everyone, confirmed by a life story I know nearly as well as my own. Milton's story reminds me then of the great importance of everyone's developmental story, how inescapable and tied it is to our daily role. We are our experience. Maybe for some a too obvious point, but nonetheless extremely important; essential to where we have been and where we are now heading. Call it a kind of psychological predestination. As children we are pointed in a particular direction, and then take off running headlong to where we don't know but actually might if we stopped a few minutes to think about it. It's that kind of predetermination I see in Milton. Fighting so hard against it, resisting with every fiber but still there he is, the child who fought against so many obstacles becoming the adult I chat and laugh with across the counter.

It's in that thought that I find my vindication in writing his story, feeling that I have accidentally put my finger on the essence, on the very pulse of this our shared human experience. Yes, you've just read Milton's story but isn't it also my story, your story, everyone's story, the unavoidable drama, sometimes melodrama that we all know?

In conclusion, I greatly encourage you to read your own personal story, to know the book that's you, rewriting it as you will, never letting it grow dusty upon some musty shelf. Become inspired, turning yourself into an anthology, adding new volume after volume, appreciating not only the quality of your current self but also of who you will someday be, whether it's next week, next month or next year, a living manuscript, a human being in perpetual development progressing onwards to your final physical breath and summation, your own death a personal exclamation point to the chapter we all are in the overall human story being composed upon the planet we share, an adventure ending when we can only guess, continued investigation our only option, and realistically, our ultimate salvation.

Milton and the author at the Tai Tung Retaurant counter.

List of Photos

Printed in the USA
CPSIA information can be obtained
at www.ICGtesting.com
LVHW092059090624
782760LV00003B/10/J